Beginner's Guide to Large Scale Model Railroading

By Marc Horovitz and Russ Larson

1	Welcome to the World of Large Scale Trains	2
2	Large Toy Trains for Kids	12
3	Ways for Adults to Enjoy Large Scale	26
4	Building an Indoor Layout	29
5	An Indoor Large Scale Empire	42
6	Introduction to Garden Railroading	48
7	Building a Garden Railroad	62
8	Large Scale Showcase	74
9	Introduction to Live Steam	80
10	Technical Information	88
	Suppliers and Organizations	95
	Index	96

First Edition
Second Printing, 1996

Published by Greenberg Books, Division of Kalmbach Publishing Co., 21027 Crossroads Circle, Waukesha, WI 53187. Telephone: (414) 796-8776.

Cataloging-in-Publication Data
Horovitz, Marc.
Beginner's guide to large scale model railroading / Marc Horovitz, Russell Larson.
p. cm.
Includes index.
ISBN 0-89778-397-2
1. Railroads—Models. I. Larson, Russell. II. Title.
TF197.H67 1994 625.1'9
QBI94-1802

CHAPTER ONE

Welcome to the World of Large Scale Trains

FIG. 1-1. This photo by Jim Forbes illustrates the size and outstanding detail characteristic of most large scale trains. The engine is an LGB model of the White Pass & Yukon's no. 110, an Alco DL535E narrow gauge diesel.

by Marc Horovitz and Russ Larson

Why are large scale trains popular today, when the trend in model railroading has traditionally been towards smaller and smaller modeling scales?

The most obvious part of the appeal is their large size. They're particularly showy and hard to ignore. Adults and children alike tend to gather around large scale trains running in malls, hobby shows, or other public places.

Because of the size and easily visible operating mechanism of large scale trains, they evoke images of the real trains they represent—big, powerful machines.

Another reason for their popularity is the fact that these big trains perform reliably. That's mainly due to the standard of quality set by the German firm of Ernst Paul Lehmann Patentwerk, which developed Lehmann's Gross Bahn (LGB), or big train—the brand that popularized large scale trains.

As a credit to LGB design, most large scale equipment will negotiate sharp curves, making it possible to operate a large scale layout in a space smaller than that required for an O scale layout. Trains made by LGB will run on curves of slightly less than 24" radius, which many serious HO scale modelers would consider minimum for their empires.

Perhaps the most significant, yet often overlooked, point of attraction to large scale trains has to do with the ability to operate them either indoors or outdoors. Large scale trains are designed to operate

FIG. 1-2. The six most commonly used modeling scales are Z, N, HO, S, O, and large scale. Large scale trains all operate on gauge 1 track, but are different scales. They are either No. 1 scale (1:32 proportion) standard gauge, or G scale (1:22.5 proportion) narrow gauge (Gn3). A Gn3 steam locomotive is shown in this photo, far right.

in a garden as well as they do around a Christmas tree!

SCALE AND GAUGE

Large scale trains come in a variety of sizes, and understanding the nuances of all the scale and gauge combinations is an intellectual exercise, which most newcomers to the hobby will not care to participate in. However, everyone modeling in large scale should understand a few basics about scale and gauge.

Scales. First, let's discuss scales. Modeling scales represent the proportion of the model to the full-size item being modeled (often called the prototype). For instance, if you build a model that is 1" = 1 foot, you're modeling in 1" scale, which has a proportion of 1:12. Likewise, a model that's ½" = 1 foot is called a ½" scale model and has a proportion of 1:24. The smaller modeling scales are represented by letters, as shown in **fig. 1-2.** In this book we'll be dealing primarily with G and No. 1 scales, whose proportions are 1:22.5 and 1:32, respectively.

Gauge. Next, you need to know about the basics of track gauge. As a beginner, you should know that this book deals with all toy and model trains that operate on gauge 1 track. Gauge 1 track has a track gauge of 45 mm (approximately 1¾") measured between the inside of the rail heads, as shown in **fig. 1-3.** Large scale trains have one thing in common—wheel spacing. They all operate on gauge 1 track.

The main difference between large scale trains is that some are models of narrow gauge prototypes, while others are models of standard gauge trains.

Except for a few tourist lines, all the trains in the United States today operate on standard gauge track, which has a spacing of 4' 8½". However, back in the late 1800s almost 20,000 miles of track was laid in the U.S. with rails spaced only 3 feet apart. These narrow gauge railroads were cheaper to construct and were the choice of many railroads serving mining towns in rugged mountain areas. They enjoyed only a brief popularity, and most were gone by the 1930s. In Europe and other parts of the world, narrow gauge railroads were built with a track gauge of 1 meter (39.37").

Fig. 1-4 shows a comparison of standard, 3-foot, and meter gauge

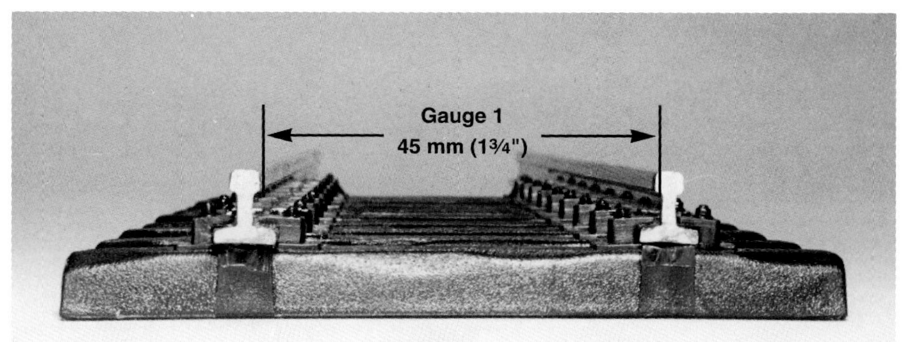

FIG. 1-3. Track gauge is measured between the inside of the rail heads.

	Scale/gauge designation	Proportion to prototype	One scale foot =	Track gauge	Approximate length of 40-foot boxcar	Minimum radius	Remarks
	Z	1:220	1.38 mm	6.5 mm	2"	5¾"	Introduced by Märklin, 1972. RTR American prototypes introduced 1985.
	N	1:160	1.9 mm	9.0 mm	3"	7½"	Developed late '60s. Second most popular scale.
	HO	1:87	3.5 mm	16.5 mm	5½"	15"	Introduced in early '30s. Grew rapidly after WWII. Most popular today.
	S	1:64	3/16"	7/8"	7½"	22½"	First commercial products, 1937. Spurred by American Flyer, 1940s, '50s.
	O	1:48	¼"	1¼"	10"	24"	Most popular scale until rise of HO. Third in popularity today.
LARGE SCALE	No. 1	1:32	3/8"	45 mm (1¾" approximately)	15"	23⅝"	Märklin European prototype. Some beautiful imported American prototype. Some live steam.
LARGE SCALE	Gn3	1:22.5	17/32"	45mm (1¾" approximately)	21¼"*	23⅝"	Introduced by Ernst Paul Lehmann in 1968. Good selection of American prototype equipment available.

* Narrow gauge boxcars were typically only 30 feet in length = 14½" in G.

track. If you're modeling in No. 1 scale (1:32), gauge 1 track is the correct spacing for standard gauge trains. If you're modeling in G scale (1:22.5), gauge 1 is correct for modeling meter gauge.

Most U.S. modelers use gauge 1 track to represent 3-foot gauge, even though a meter is just over 3" wider than 3 feet. The term Gn3 is sometimes used as a way to describe this scale-gauge combination, even though the term is somewhat of a misnomer. The G stands for G scale, the n for narrow gauge, and the 3 for 3-foot. Technically, the term should be Gnm or just Gm for G scale, meter gauge.

Narrow gauge railroad equipment was smaller than standard gauge. Keep that in mind as we

FIG. 1-4. The diagram below compares standard gauge track to both European (1-meter) narrow gauge and U. S. (3-foot) narrow gauge.

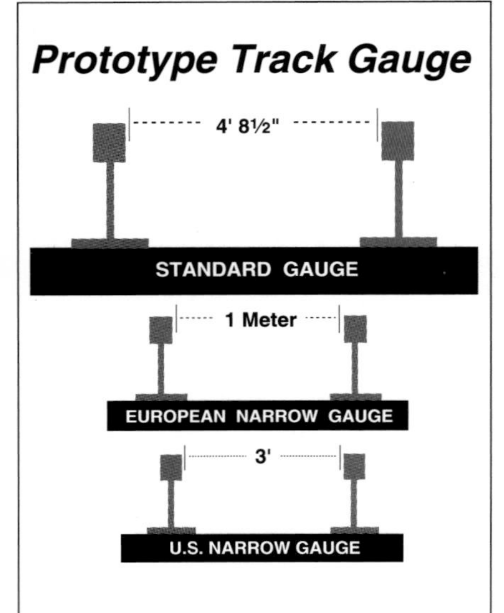

FIG. 1-5. Railroads were built in the U.S. with both narrow and standard track gauges. Where a narrow gauge line interchanged with a standard gauge line, dual gauge track was common. Here we see an East Broad Top standard gauge switch engine pulling a string of narrow gauge hopper cars on dual gauge track. Photo taken in 1953 by Philip R. Hastings.

look at the two types of models offered in large scale.

Narrow gauge models. The LGB line, introduced in 1968, features models of narrow gauge trains from around the world. The proportion of the models to the real trains is 1:22.5, or a little bigger than ½" = 1 foot. This scale has been designated G for Garden or the German word *Gross* (big). Because these are models of narrow gauge trains, *Model Railroader* magazine uses the designation Gn3.

Standard gauge models. Some manufacturers offer models of standard gauge equipment with wheels spaced to operate on gauge 1 track. Those built to a proportion of 1:32 are called No. 1 scale models.

Earlier, we pointed out that real narrow gauge locomotives and cars were smaller than standard gauge equipment. Therefore, a narrow gauge model and standard gauge model of the same rail car, although built to different scales, will be approximately the same physical size, as shown in **fig. 1-6.**

In summary, there are two basic types of large scale trains:

- Gn3 (1:22.5 proportion) models of narrow gauge trains.
- No. 1 scale (1:32 proportion) models of standard gauge trains.

Many people don't really care whether a model is based on a narrow or standard gauge prototype. They enjoy mixing the equipment on their layouts. However, if you tend towards accurate modeling, you'll want to read more about this subject.

HISTORICAL NOTES

The model train hobby can trace its origins to the beginning of the full-size railroad industry in the 1830s. For decades, in fact, the development of model railways paralleled that of full-size railways. Railroad builders often built models to test theories and to present their ideas to an adoring public.

The first primitive model trains were made by craftsmen for themselves or for wealthy clients. Since they were most often powered by steam and fairly large in scale, they were operated outdoors.

It wasn't long before manufacturers got the notion that there might be a few dollars to be made making toy trains. The toy train makers sprouted like weeds, primarily in Germany and Great Britain. Nearly everyone who had even the slightest metalworking skills began making toy and model trains to greater or lesser degrees of sophistication.

As a result of the great number of manufacturers in the model train industry, there was no continuity in scale of the trains or gauge of the

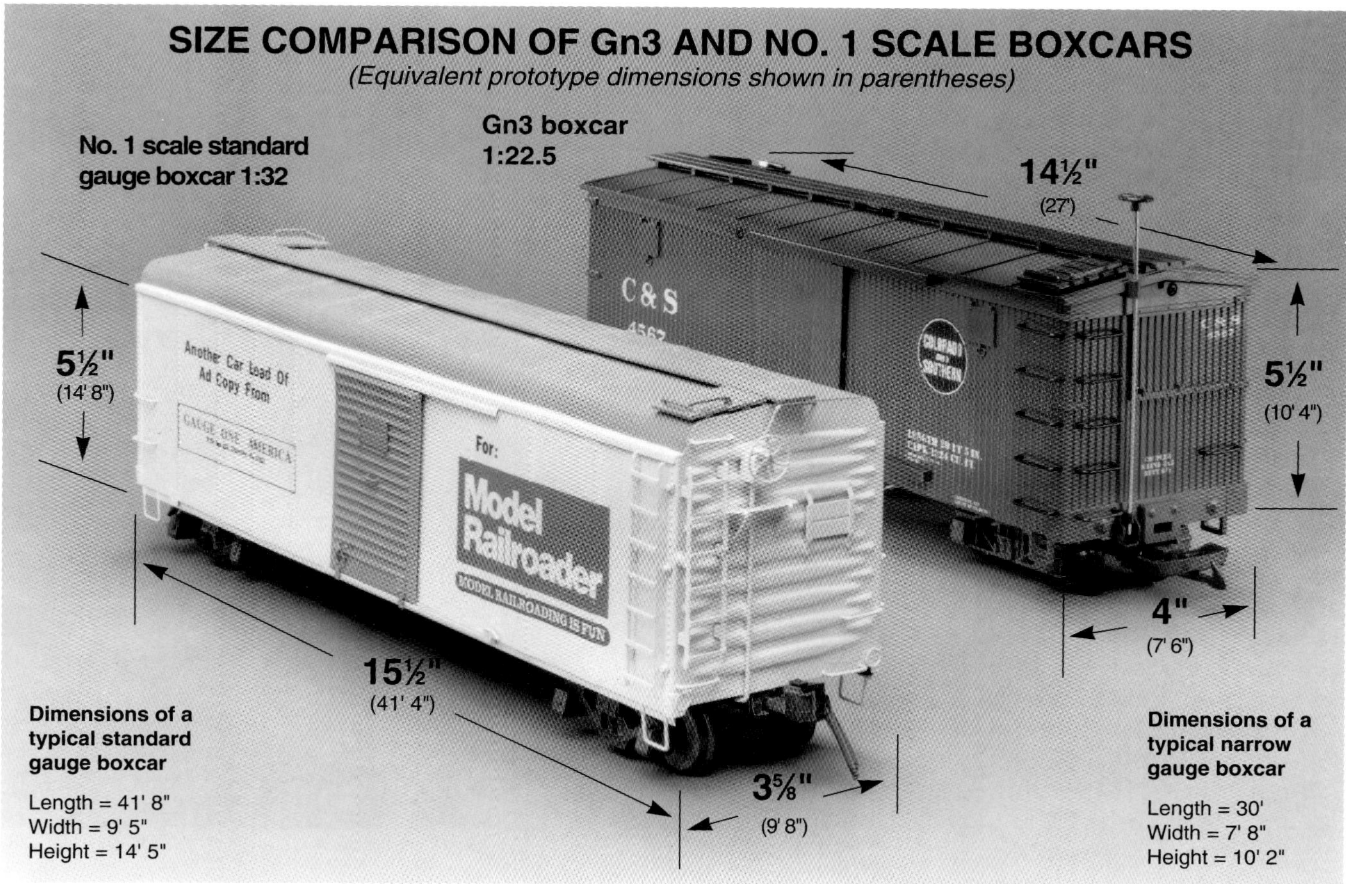

FIG. 1-6. Gn3 & No. 1 scale boxcars, sizes compared.

FIG. 1-7. This Ives O gauge windup (clockwork) locomotive was introduced in 1921. Photo by A. L. Schmidt.

track. If I wanted to run my trains on your track, chances were pretty good that I couldn't, due to the disparity in the gauges of our track.

Märklin's track standards. This state of affairs ended in the late 1880s, when the famous and still-extant Märklin company of Germany set forth standardized gauges and scales. Their first three offerings were imaginatively named gauge 1, gauge 2, and gauge 3. Gauge 1, at 45 mm, was the smallest, and gauge 3, at 62 mm, was the largest. These standards were soon adopted by virtually all European and some American model train manufacturers.

By today's standards, even the small gauge 1 was still fairly large. Few people had enough space to build a gauge 1 railway indoors, so they built them *outdoors.* The more sophisticated builders molded the terrain through which their trains ran, and added suitable plants and vegetation to enhance their lines. Eventually the term garden railway came to be used to describe this type of outdoor model railroad.

Toy and model train manufacturers soon realized that by producing trains that were too large for indoor use and too expensive for most people to afford, they were limiting their market. So a new, smaller standardized scale-gauge combination was introduced. Since there were no appropriate numbers left, the new gauge—32 mm between the rails—was given zero as its designation. What we now refer to as O (oh) gauge is technically the original zero gauge. An early gauge 0 locomotive is shown in **fig. 1-7.**

Gauge 0 took off like wildfire and soon eclipsed the larger sizes. It could be used indoors or out; the engines could be powered by old-fashioned steam or clockwork, or newfangled electricity; and the trains were cheap enough that anyone who wanted a railway could have one.

Meanwhile, out in the garden, gauge 1 was still the accepted favorite. Several large railways sprang up on British estates, and smaller ones were created in more modest environs. Gauge 0 was used as well, sometimes by children who brought their Hornby or Bassett-Lowke trains outdoors to build railways that varied in permanence.

Lionel's influence. In the United States, though, things were different. Gauge 1 never had a great following. The Lionel Corporation (followed by the American Flyer Company and others) developed their own large gauge, which they called Standard gauge. (See **fig. 1-8.**) Standard gauge track measured 2⅛" between the rails and fit no common scale.

For decades during the first part of the twentieth century, Lionel was the leading supplier of toy trains in America. Virtually *all* of their literature promoted the use of the trains indoors. Lionel was such a formidable influence in the industry that they as much as dictated how the trains were to be used. In those years

FIG. 1-8. This layout table of toy train collector Ward Kimball has loops of track that are O, nos. 1 and 2, Standard, and 2⅞" gauge. Steam locomotive no. 4670 pulling the orange passenger cars is American Flyer Standard gauge. Photo by Andy Sperandeo.

FIG. 1-9. The nonpowered Buddy "L" outdoor railroad was big enough and rugged enough that children could ride on the cars. This Buddy "L" garden line was constructed in the early 1930s by Leonard Cooper for his son Richard. It survives today and still runs with the original rolling stock. Unpowered Buddy "L" locomotives were modified and powered to run off a center third rail. Some of the rolling stock, like the snowplow, is scratchbuilt, while other is stock Buddy "L."

garden railroading had little chance.

During the 1920s and '30s, American Flyer and a few others minimally advertised their products for use outdoors. There was, of course, the famous Buddy "L" nonpowered railway system, designed expressly for outdoor use. However, this large, expensive system saw relatively small acceptance, despite the ruggedness and beauty of the trains. (See **fig. 1-9.**)

Garden railways were sometimes featured in U.S. railroad and model railroad publications during the first half of the century, though they were most often presented as a novelty. In Britain and other parts of the world, garden railways were more a part of the mainstream pastime of model railroading, and they were prominently featured in the industry press.

One notable American exception was the garden line called Ganesha Junction, shown in **fig. 1-10.** It was built for the City of Los Angeles at the Los Angeles County Fairgrounds in Pomona. The roots of this ½" scale, gauge 3 (2½" gauge) line go back to the late 1920s. This railroad still operates annually during the fair.

Smaller-size trains dominate. The demise of large scale railroads—both indoors and out—was drawing near by the time World War II came along. By the end of the war, gauge 1 was obsolete, and gauge 2 and 3 had long since died out. New, smaller scales were becoming popular. They allowed much more railroad to be built in a given space.

The smaller scales were particularly attractive to those hobbyists who were starting new families and didn't have a lot of extra room.

Ironically, at this low ebb in the hobby's history, the first book was published that really combined gardening and model railroads into what we know today as garden railroading. *Garden Railways,* written by R. E. Tustin (**fig. 1-11**), and published by Percival Marshall in Britain in 1949, told us how to build the railway as well as how to successfully integrate it into the garden. This book, which is still in great demand, is surprisingly current today.

0 gauge would still be popular for a few more years. By attrition it had become the largest scale commonly available. In the United States, Lionel was still very much in the forefront with its 0 gauge trains. In the late '40s and early '50s nearly every small boy wanted a Lionel train, and many got them.

In the United States, large scale railroads were almost unheard of throughout the 1950s and 1960s. They were out of favor in Britain during this period also, but because they had been more popular in that country earlier in the century, they still existed in some numbers.

FIG. 1-10. One of the oldest garden railways in this country, the Ganesha Junction was begun in the late 1920s. This 2½" gauge, ½" scale line resides at the Los Angeles County Fairgrounds in Pomona, California. Trains are all scratchbuilt and electrically powered. Photo by Marc Horovitz.

FIG. 1-11: ***The late R. E. Tustin is considered by many to be the father of modern-day garden railroading. His treatise on the subject,*** **Garden Railways,** ***was published in 1949 and contains much information that is still relevant today. Tustin is seen here with his O scale line in Britain. Both the garden and the railway have been raised by the use of a stone wall for ease of access and viewing. The railway's rockery plants put on quite a show for spring. Photo by Marc Horovitz.***

LGB is born. In 1968 the German toymaking company of Ernst Paul Lehmann introduced a new concept in model trains. Their all-plastic products were initially models of narrow gauge trains from Germany. They were built to the heretofore unheard-of scale of 1:22.5, and they ran on the old standardized gauge 1 track. The LGB trains were specifically designed for use outdoors. They were rugged, and all of the more fragile gears and motor parts were encapsulated to keep them free of dirt.

LGB's product line constituted a revolution in model railroading—one that did not succeed overnight. Since the trains were brightly colored models of European equipment, most "serious" modelers in the U.S. viewed them as toys. But Lehmann persevered, and the company continued to develop new products based on narrow-gauge railroads from around the world.

Eventually, articles on the potential of these trains in both indoor and outdoor environments began to appear in model train magazines. The late Charles Small, a noted railroad author, wrote about the outdoor use of LGB trains for *Model Railroader* in the mid 1970s ("Charles Small's LG&B RR," *Model Railroader*, April 1972). The flame was kindled.

Small live steamers. Meanwhile, a revolution was occurring in Britain as well. Small live-steam locomotives—engines that actually ran on fire and water—had been popular in years past, but interest had all but died out during the 1950s. In the late 1960s and early 1970s a new company called Archangel, headed by Stewart Browne, revived interest in these small steamers.

Up until this time the small steam locomotive could be a very temperamental thing indeed. It either ran at 90 miles per hour until the fuel was exhausted, or it required the same constant attention that was necessary to operate a full-sized locomotive.

Stewart reasoned that if he could come up with a locomotive that would run at a sedate speed for a reasonable amount of time, and that didn't cost an arm and a leg, he'd have a winner. And he did, on all counts.

Archangel models were generally of narrow gauge proportions, built to the scale of 16 mm to the foot to run on gauge 0 track. They were big and heavy, and they lacked certain refinements, but they were colorful, powerful, and docile.

In the mid '70s, the Aster Company of Japan began producing live-steam locomotives that ran on gauge 1 track. These models were usually standard gauge in 1:32 proportion (No. 1 scale). Today they are the largest producer of small live-steam models. Their range of engines has run the gamut from a tiny 0-4-0T to a model of the Union Pacific 4-8-8-4 Big Boy. (See **fig. 1-12.**) In recent

FIG. 1-12. An Aster live steam Union Pacific 4-8-8-4 Big Boy pulls a freight across a trestle at a garden railway display at the Ohio State Fair. Other Aster live steamers can be seen in the background. Photo by Jim Hediger.

years Aster has also produced electrically powered models.

A Gauge One Model Railway Association was formed in the early 1960s; it is alive and well today. LGB has prospered. And today several large American companies (including Aristo-Craft, Bachmann, Lionel, and USA Trains) make large scale trains, following LGB's precepts. To complement these manufacturers, dozens of small companies and cottage industries are now putting out related products that make modelers happy and keep the industry hard at work.

In 1984 *Garden Railways* magazine began publication. Edited by Marc and Barbara Horovitz, the publication stresses integrating the railway with a garden to achieve a railway-like atmosphere. It is the only model train magazine that has regular gardening articles and its own garden editor.

Though large scale railroading as practiced today is much different from what it was a hundred years ago, its roots can be easily traced, and the influence of the past masters can be clearly seen in today's more sophisticated railways.

WHAT'S HAPPENING TODAY

Today, large scale is a rapidly growing segment of the model railroad hobby. While G scale trains have been available in the U.S. since the early 1970s, those initially offered were models of European trains and thus of limited interest.

Then in 1985, LGB introduced a 2-6-0 (Mogul) based on a real Colorado narrow gauge prototype. It was impressive! (See **fig. 1-13.**) Besides the engine, appropriate freight and passenger cars were offered, along with typical structures from the Old West by Pola, another German firm. With U.S. prototype trains available, interest in large scale took off like a runaway train.

Since then a whole line of products has developed, and other firms have offered models operating on gauge 1 track, in both narrow and standard gauge.

Interest in large scale trains is being expressed in a number of ways. Many veteran model railroaders are finding large scale to be

FIG. 1-13. LGB's first U.S. prototype locomotive was this colorful Mogul, introduced in 1985. As the comparison with the real Denver, South Park & Pacific engine shows, it's a very accurate scale model. Photos: R. H. Kindig collection (above) and A. L. Schmidt (below).

an enjoyable addition to their interest in smaller scales. For some, large scale has made model railroading a year-around hobby. In the winter they enjoy working on an N or HO scale layout. Then in the summer they enjoy large scale trains outdoors in a garden railroad. (See **fig. 1-14.**)

Large scale trains are also attracting new people to model railroading. They begin by buying a large scale train set and put a loop of track around the Christmas tree. This leads to the purchase of more track and turnouts, and experimentation begins with various track arrangements. Then interest builds and plans begin to form for a permanent indoor or outdoor layout.

Whether you're a veteran model railroader who has just discovered large scale trains or a complete newcomer to model trains, you'll find useful information in this book.

First, we'll give you some suggestions as to how you and children of all ages can enjoy large scale trains together. Next, we'll look at ways adults enjoy these big model trains. If you have a spare room, attic, garage, or basement, we'll help you get started building a model railroad empire complete with scenery, structures, vehicles, people—all the things you'd find in real life.

FIG. 1-14. Veteran model railroader Bob Kelley spent 20 years working in HO scale before discovering Gn3 in 1985. Now he spends most of his modeling time working on a garden railroad he calls The Longwood, Geneva & Bellisle (LGB). Photo by Bob Kelley.

FIG. 1-15. A good selection of reliable live steam locomotives that operate on gauge 1 track is available. This little 0-4-0 puffing along on Grover Devine's garden railway was kitbashed from an engine made in Great Britain by Merlin Locomotive Works. Photo by George Hall.

If you want to try something different, how about large scale outdoors? We'll show you how to build a garden railroad—an adventure combining some of the challenges of building a real railroad with the joys of flower gardening.

Then there's live steam. Several brands of steam-powered locomotives are offered that operate on gauge 1 track. And these little cookers can be controlled by radio. (See **fig. 1-15.**) It's a lot of fun!

Large scale trains are also collectible. Some people want to buy every piece produced by a certain manufacturer. Others try to figure out what items will appreciate in value in the future. Still others just buy what appeals to them and display the models for their own enjoyment. (See **fig. 1-16.**)

These big trains are fun for kids and they can be the catalyst for parent-child bonding. You can enjoy large scale as an adjunct to your interest in smaller scale trains. Or they can become your main hobby as you build and refine either an indoor or outdoor model railroad. Finally, you may be interested in these beautiful models as collectibles that you buy, sell, swap, and display.

FIG. 1-16. John Gummo, an importer of large scale brass models, has an extensive collection beautifully displayed. Collecting large scale models can be an adjunct to the hobby of building and operating a layout, or a hobby unto itself. Photo by Chris Becker.

CHAPTER TWO

Large Toy Trains For Kids

FIG. 2-1. The mutual interest in large scale trains can provide the catalyst for parent-child bonding.

by Russ Larson

There was a time, in the 1940s and '50s, when every American boy dreamed of receiving a Lionel or American Flyer train set for Christmas, along with such other favorite boy's toys as a Daisy BB gun or a Red Ryder coaster wagon.

Maybe you picked up this book because you loved the train set you had as a child. Well, nostalgia is great, but what about today's children? Do they want a train set as a gift? It's doubtful that they'll ask for one, because that's not what is advertised on children's TV programs. But I can almost guarantee you that if they receive a train set, it will quickly become one of their favorite toys.

Here's a test you can conduct to see if your child or grandchild likes trains: Take the child to a train show or a hobby shop that has an operating display and watch his or her reaction to the trains. Almost every major city (and many small ones) has at least an annual train show like the one shown in **fig. 2-2.** For information on shows in your area, ask at your local hobby shop or consult the Schedules listing in each issue of the magazines *Model Railroader* and *Classic Toy Trains.*

Whenever I attend train shows, I watch the children watch the trains. When young children see trains running, their eyes light up, they laugh or smile, or they just get excited. They love watching the trains! It seems to be almost instinctive, because many of today's children haven't ridden on a real train. Some have never even seen a real train except on TV!

But then I guess the connection with real trains isn't really necessary because toy and model trains are appealing in and of themselves. After all, they're big (especially to a small child), colorful, and noisy. They glide around the track in a seemingly purposeful manner, and they're remotely controlled. If the locomotives smoke and make sounds like a real one, and the layout has operating accessories, so much the better.

Imagine what a thrill it must be for a 4- or 5-year-old to be able to control a big train's speed, direction, and route. A "child" of any age can truly appreciate this power!

LARGE TRAINS FOR SMALL CHILDREN

Large toy trains are ideal for small children. They're almost indestructible—the main criterion for play by boys and girls from around 4 to 7 years old. These big trains are more likely to stay on the track during rough play than their smaller cousins in N, HO, and O scales. And they're easier for younger children to rerail when necessary.

I don't mean to imply that these big trains are just good for young

FIG. 2-2. Attending a train show is a good way to find out if that favorite child in your life likes trains. Almost every major city has at least one such show annually. Photo by Russ Larson.

AGES 1-3

Push and pull toys for tots

AGES 4-7

Large-size electric trains with adult supervision

AGES 8-11

Large, rugged electric trains

AGE 12 AND OLDER

Any size trains are suitable

FIG. 2-3. Children at different ages will enjoy different kinds of trains.

children. They're for older children and adults too. But older folks have the patience and dexterity to be able to choose any scale and gauge combination from Z to G. **Fig. 2-3** provides guidelines for selecting trains for children of various ages.

Adult supervision. Because the trains operate from a power pack that plugs into a 110-volt outlet, a responsible parent will supervise the play of young children or devise some way to make the power pack inaccessible to the children. It's the 110-volt line cord that you have to worry about. The 12 to 18 volts DC output from the pack that powers the trains is not dangerous.

Another reason for adult supervision is that the locomotives are heavy. A small switching locomotive weighs about 3 pounds and a large steam locomotive can weigh up to 8 pounds. That's too heavy for a very small child to lift. Even if they can lift it, they might drop it and injure themselves.

WHAT'S AVAILABLE?

You can buy a locomotive, a selection of cars, a power pack, and some track separately at a hobby shop. However, you'll get a better price by buying a complete train set that includes all these necessary ingredients in one package.

Large scale trains and accessories are available year round at hobby shops. I'd encourage you to visit one near you to get an idea of the variety of products available in large scale. (See **fig. 2-4.**) A few shops even specialize in large scale.

Large scale train sets are also sold through toy store chains such as Toys "R" Us, Children's Palace, and Kay Bee Toys. The best selection at toy stores is during the Christmas selling season. Large scale trains are also sold by mail-order firms that advertise in magazines like *Garden Railways, Classic Toy Trains,* and *Model Railroader.*

In general, large scale train sets are of pretty good quality. LGB large scale toy trains have a well-deserved reputation for outstanding

FIG. 2-4. By visiting a well-stocked hobby shop, you'll get a good overview of what's available in large scale. This will help you plan the type of layout you want to build for your child or yourself. Photo by Roger Carp features Alice Morris, proprietor of H & R Hobbies, St. Petersburg, Florida.

quality. Large scale toy trains offered by Bachmann, Aristo-Craft, Lionel, Playmobil, and others are fine products that will provide years of trouble-free service. A sampling of large scale train sets from various manufacturers is shown in **fig. 2-5.**

Train sets are sold in colorful packages. Before making a purchasing decision, look beyond the beautiful color photo or artwork and read the fine print to see what the box actually contains. Make sure a power pack and track are included in addition to the train. And see how many cars are included. You may want to purchase a few extra cars because a one- or two-car train isn't very interesting to watch.

The most important single item in a train set is the locomotive. A faulty engine will quickly take the fun out of this toy, so ask to test the locomotive before you buy the set. Many hobby shops have a test track where you can do this. If you buy at some other outlet, be sure to keep your receipt and do your own test as soon as you get home.

Connecting the power pack. Some type of track connectors come with most train sets. If not, purchase a set of LGB's track power terminals (5016/1). You have to run two wires from the power pack to the track. Connect one end of a no. 20 or larger (smaller gauge number) wire to one variable DC terminal of your power pack and the other to one rail. Connect another length of no. 20 wire to the other variable DC terminal and the other rail. (See **fig. 2-6.**)

TRAIN SET CHECKLIST

- Read the instructions.
- Examine the contents for any obvious damage in shipment.

FIG. 2-5. A large scale train set is a good gift for a child who shows an interest in toy trains. A train set includes a locomotive, several cars, an oval of track, a power pack, and sometimes other accessories. The three sets shown are a Playmobil steam passenger set (above, left), an LGB steam freight set (above), and a Bachmann Big Hauler set (left).

- Assemble the track.
- Connect wires from the power pack to the track.
- Plug in the power pack.
- Place locomotive on the track.
- Turn up the power pack and see if the locomotive runs.
- Finally, place the remaining consist of cars on the track and test to see if the complete train runs without excessive effort or derailments.

TRACK ARRANGEMENTS

Playing trains is fun, and it can be educational too. Children can learn how to solve problems, improve their manual dexterity and eye-hand coordination, and discover how to share and cooperate with others.

How much a child gains from his or her trains depends on the arrangement of track, the buildings, figures, and accessories used, and the child's imagination.

The track that comes with the set will be enough to make a circle or oval. And that's a good way to begin. Let the child enjoy watching the train go around and around. He or she will enjoy controlling the speed and direction of the trains for a while, but even a small child will soon tire of this. Then it's time to make things more interesting by

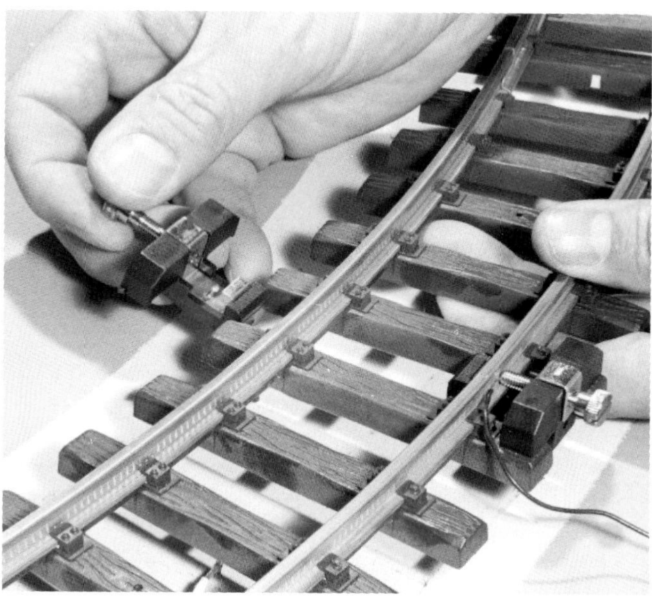

Step 1.

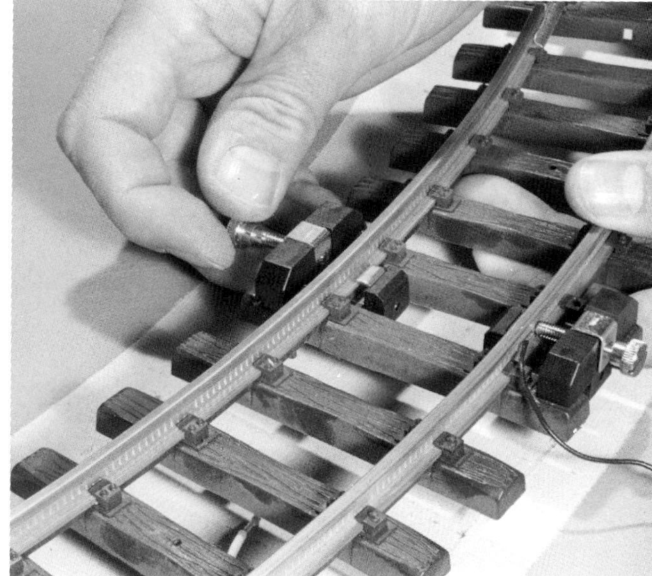

Step 2.

Step 3.

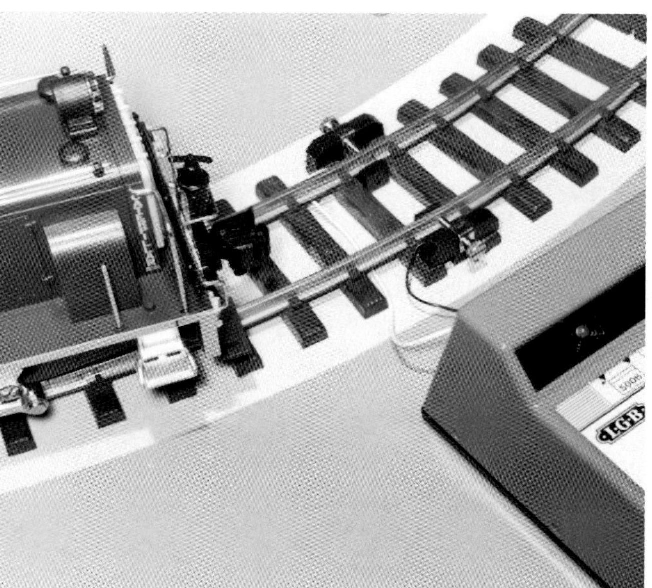

Step 4.

FIG. 2-6. Connecting wires from the power pack to the rails. Steps 1 and 2: Slip the terminals under the rail. Step 3: Run a wire with the insulation stripped off the end along the outside of the rail and tighten the terminal screw pinching the wire against the rail. Step 4: Now you're ready to run trains. Art Schmidt photos.

buying some more track and changing the track configuration. Add a few turnouts, so the routing of the train can be varied, and things get really interesting.

The plans shown in **fig. 2-7** offer a small sampling of the many track arrangements possible. Most of these plans feature variations of the basic loop, but don't dismiss the back-and-forth setup (what model railroaders call point-to-point), since it can be permanently mounted on a shelf and doesn't take up much space. A child can have just as much fun, and maybe more, running trains back and forth while doing a little switching. LGB offers an Automatic Shuttle Circuit (no. 0090), which enables you to set up an automatic back-and-forth operation with realistic stops and starts.

FIG. 2-7. Seven different track arrangements are shown below and on the next page using LGB track.

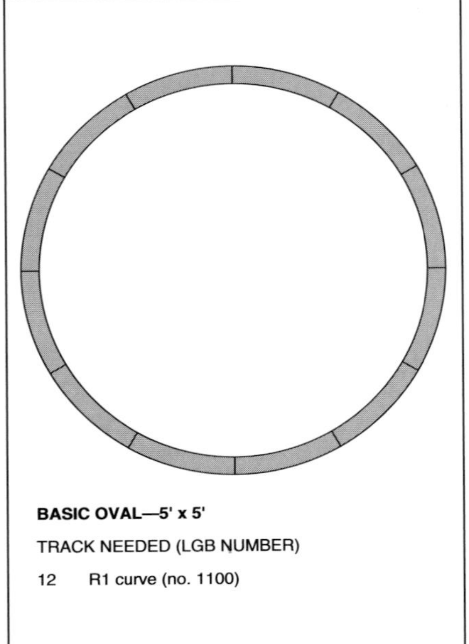

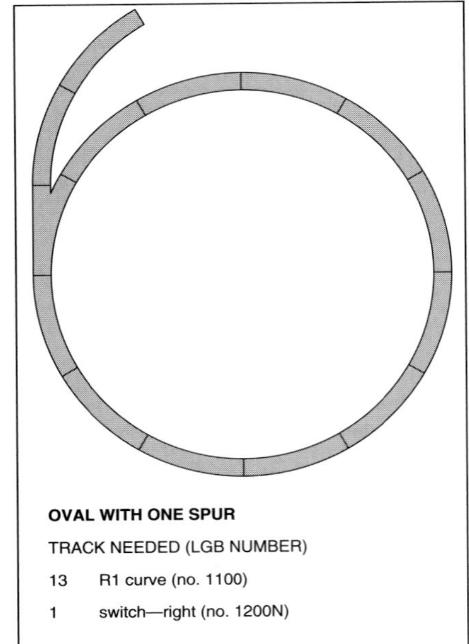

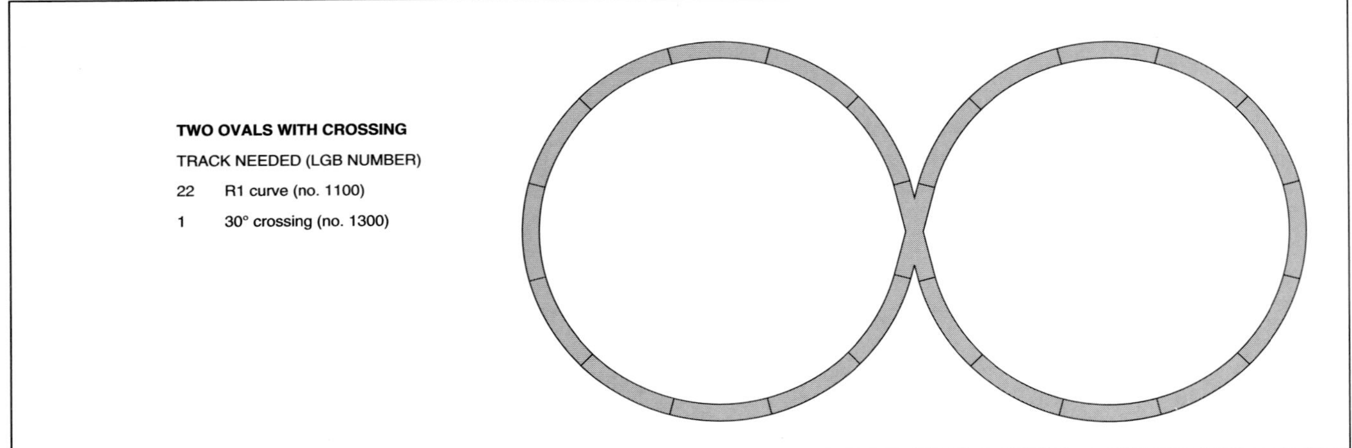

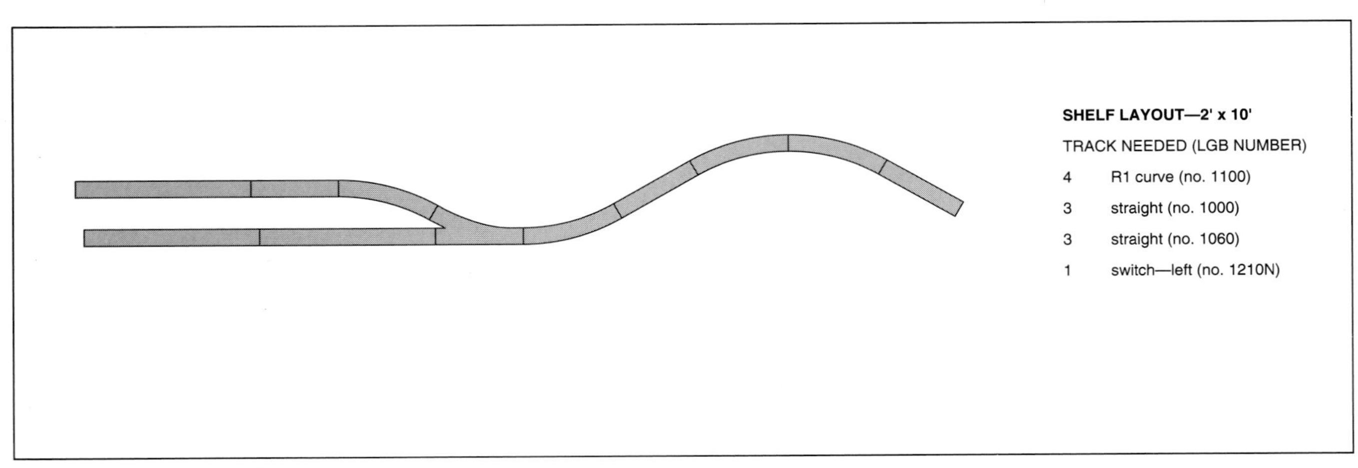

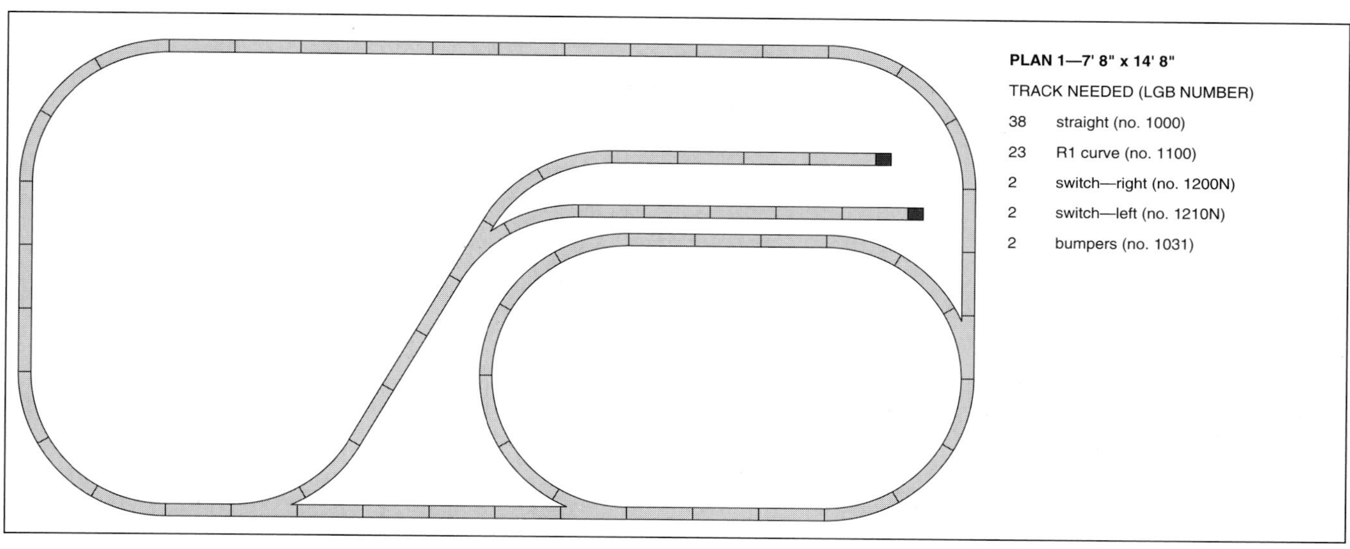
PLAN 1—7' 8" x 14' 8"
TRACK NEEDED (LGB NUMBER)
38 straight (no. 1000)
23 R1 curve (no. 1100)
2 switch—right (no. 1200N)
2 switch—left (no. 1210N)
2 bumpers (no. 1031)

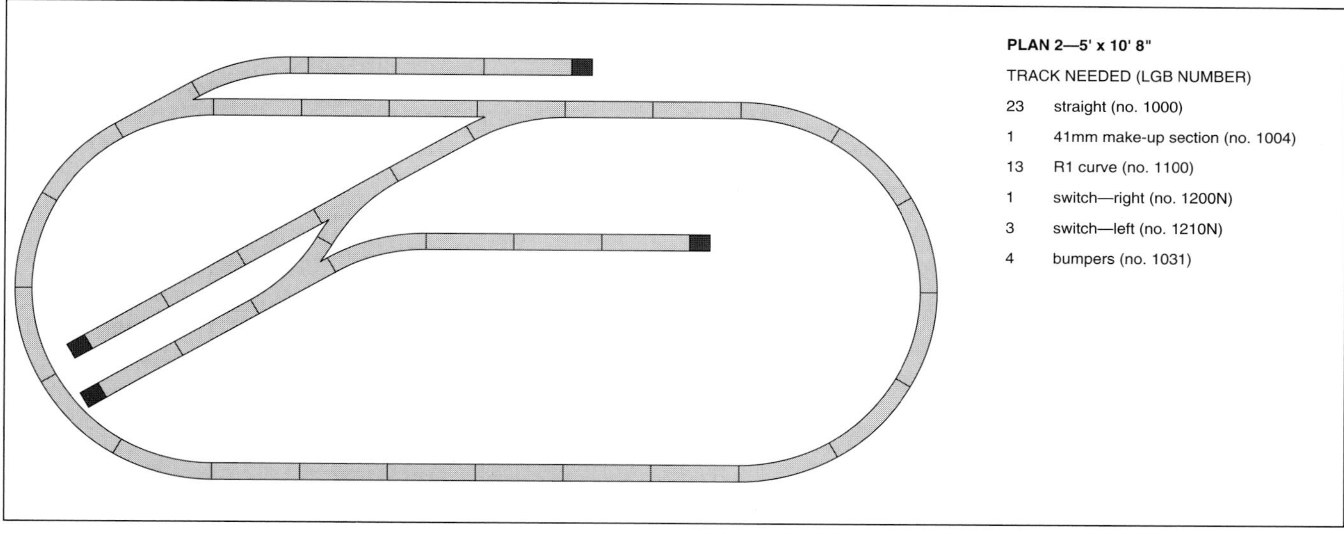
PLAN 2—5' x 10' 8"
TRACK NEEDED (LGB NUMBER)
23 straight (no. 1000)
1 41mm make-up section (no. 1004)
13 R1 curve (no. 1100)
1 switch—right (no. 1200N)
3 switch—left (no. 1210N)
4 bumpers (no. 1031)

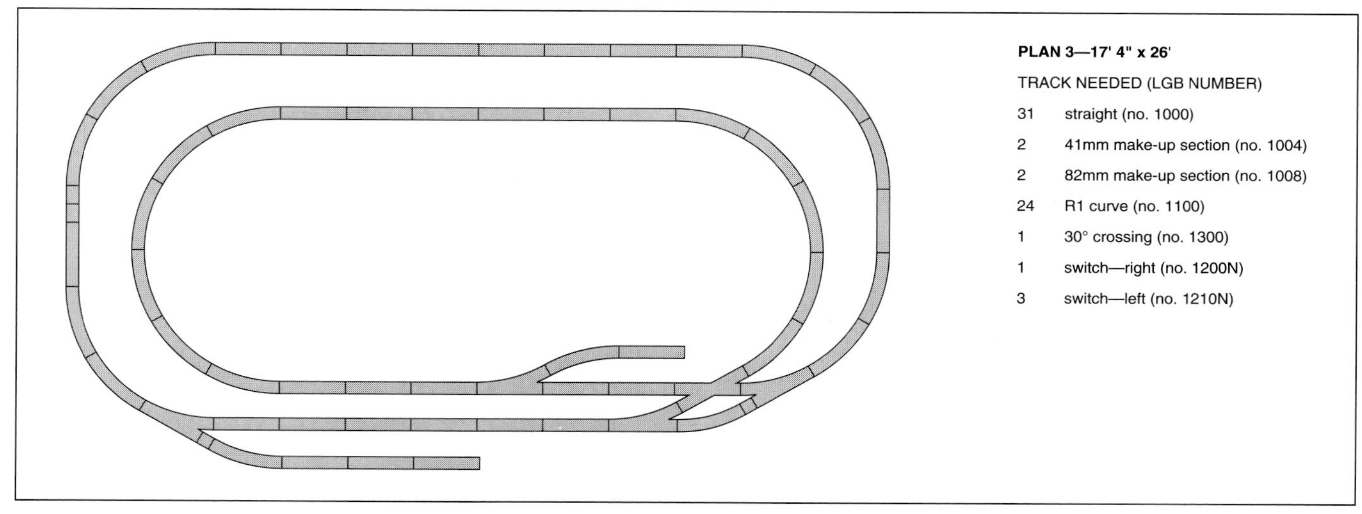
PLAN 3—17' 4" x 26'
TRACK NEEDED (LGB NUMBER)
31 straight (no. 1000)
2 41mm make-up section (no. 1004)
2 82mm make-up section (no. 1008)
24 R1 curve (no. 1100)
1 30° crossing (no. 1300)
1 switch—right (no. 1200N)
3 switch—left (no. 1210N)

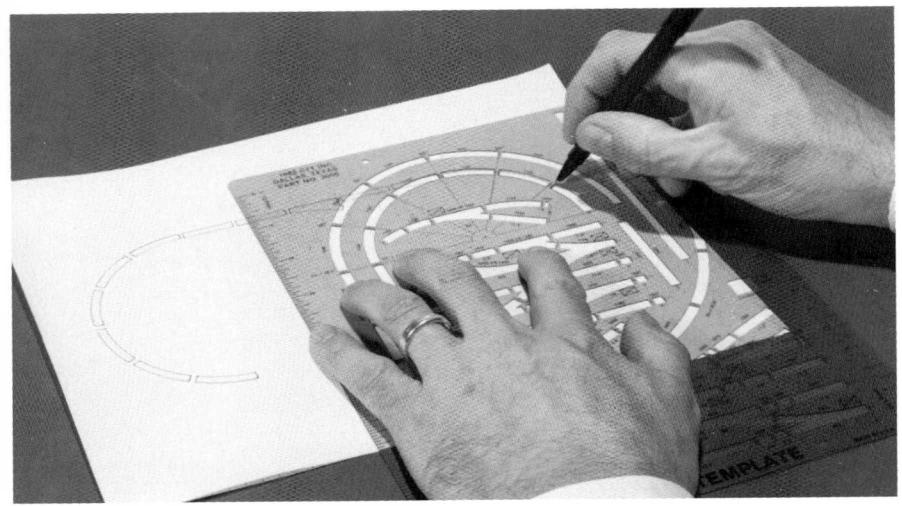

FIG. 2-8. You can design your own track plans with a template like this one by CTT. LGB offers a track-planing template too. Art Schmidt photo.

All the plans specify LGB track because at the time of this writing it's the most widely available brand with the best selection of track radii, turnout sizes, and crossings. Of course, similar plans can be built with other brands, as well. Check at your local hobby shop to see what's currently available.

You can design your own track plan. With the aid of a track-planning template like the one shown in **fig. 2-8,** it's quite easy and enjoyable. LGB offers a track-planning template, as does a firm called CTT Inc.

As you're experimenting with different track plans, you'll probably simply snap the track pieces together on the floor as shown in **fig. 2-9.** And there's nothing wrong with continuing to set up the track each time your child wants to play with the trains. Just be sure to avoid setting up the track on deep-pile carpeting like shag, as carpet fuzz may accumulate around the wheels of cars and locomotives and cause problems.

TRAIN BOARDS

Eventually you'll hit upon a track plan that your child finds interesting, and you'll be putting the track together and taking it apart quite frequently. When you grow tired of doing that, it's time to think about mounting the track to a train board.

When the track is mounted to a board, the "layout," like the one shown in **fig. 2-10,** is ready to use at a moment's notice. Having the track mounted also eliminates potential electrical problems at the rail joints and enables you to get the track up off the floor to a height where the kids can view the trains from a more realistic angle. And Dad and Mom can "supervise" from the comfort of a chair too. This is the first step towards building a full-fledged model railroad layout with structures and scenery.

FIG. 2-9. Children can have a lot of fun with a temporary train layout set up on the floor like this. Simply snap the track together and run two wires from the power pack to track connectors. Photo courtesy LGB.

FIG. 2-10. When you hit upon a track arrangement the kids like, mount the track on a train board. This train board consists of two interior doors joined by hinges so that it can be folded up when not in use. Art Schmidt photo.

Step 1.

Step 2.

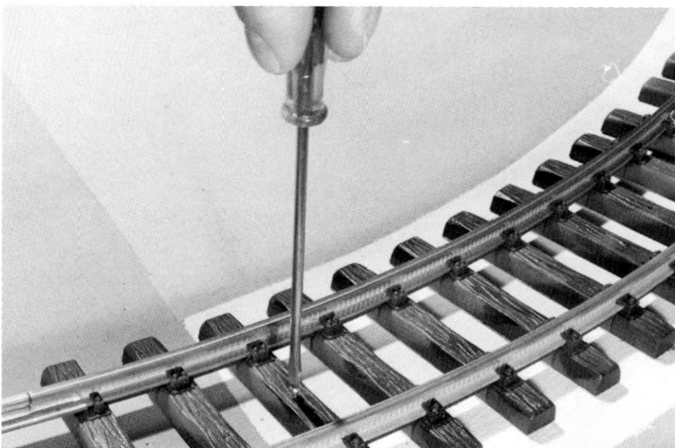

Step 3.

FIG. 2-11. Track can be fastened to a train board with no. 4 screws, 1/2" long. Step 1: Drill a 1/16" pilot hole. Step 2: Insert the screw. Step 3: Drive it home using a small screwdriver. Art Schmidt photos.

Fastening track. The track can be fastened to the board using no. 3 or 4 x ½" screws, as shown in **fig. 2-11.** Drilling 1/16" pilot holes will make the installation easier.

You can also fasten the track using no. 19 wire brads at least ½" long. If you're mounting the track to a fiber board, you may need to drill no. 61 pilot holes first. Place a dab of white glue on the tip of the brad to ensure that it will stay in place.

There are many types of train boards. The simplest of all is a sheet of plywood set on two sawhorses. If you include some framing and legs, you will have a train board that can grow to become a small model railroad.

INCREASING THE PLAY VALUE

The plan shown in **fig. 2-13** is designed to fit a 5 x 9 board, which just happens to be the size of a Ping-Pong table. In fact, if you happen to have an old Ping-Pong table it will make a nice train board. Many Ping-Pong tables fold up for convenient storage. If yours does, you'll want to include LGB's expandable track sections at the joints, so that the track can be easily retracted when you want to fold up the train board.

You can build the plan shown in fig. 2-13 on a 5 x 9-foot train board that you have made from a sheet of 4 x 8 and a sheet of 2 x 8 plywood. There are some things you can add to the train board that will make "playing trains" more fun. Let's add to our basic Ping-Pong Railroad to enhance its play value a few sidings, a station, and some industrial buildings, as well as some uncoupling ramps, some people, and animals.

Kits for G scale buildings are expensive, so you might consider making your own to begin with. Use cardboard boxes and draw on some windows and doors. Your child's imagination will do the rest.

With these additions, the train board is visually more attractive and more interesting as a toy. Now we can challenge the child to solve a few problems.

For example, in the setup shown in **fig. 2-14,** ask the child to switch the boxcar into the siding marked "x." To do that he or she must do what's called a runaround. It's fun!

Toy trains provide only part of the equation. The minds of the children provide the rest. Children must imagine what's not there—buildings, people, cars. They'll make up stories to explain why they're doing what they're doing with the trains.

A good way to stimulate a young child's imagination is by reading illustrated stories to him or her (**fig. 2-15**). There are some good children's books about trains. For example, a modern version of the venerable *The Little Engine That*

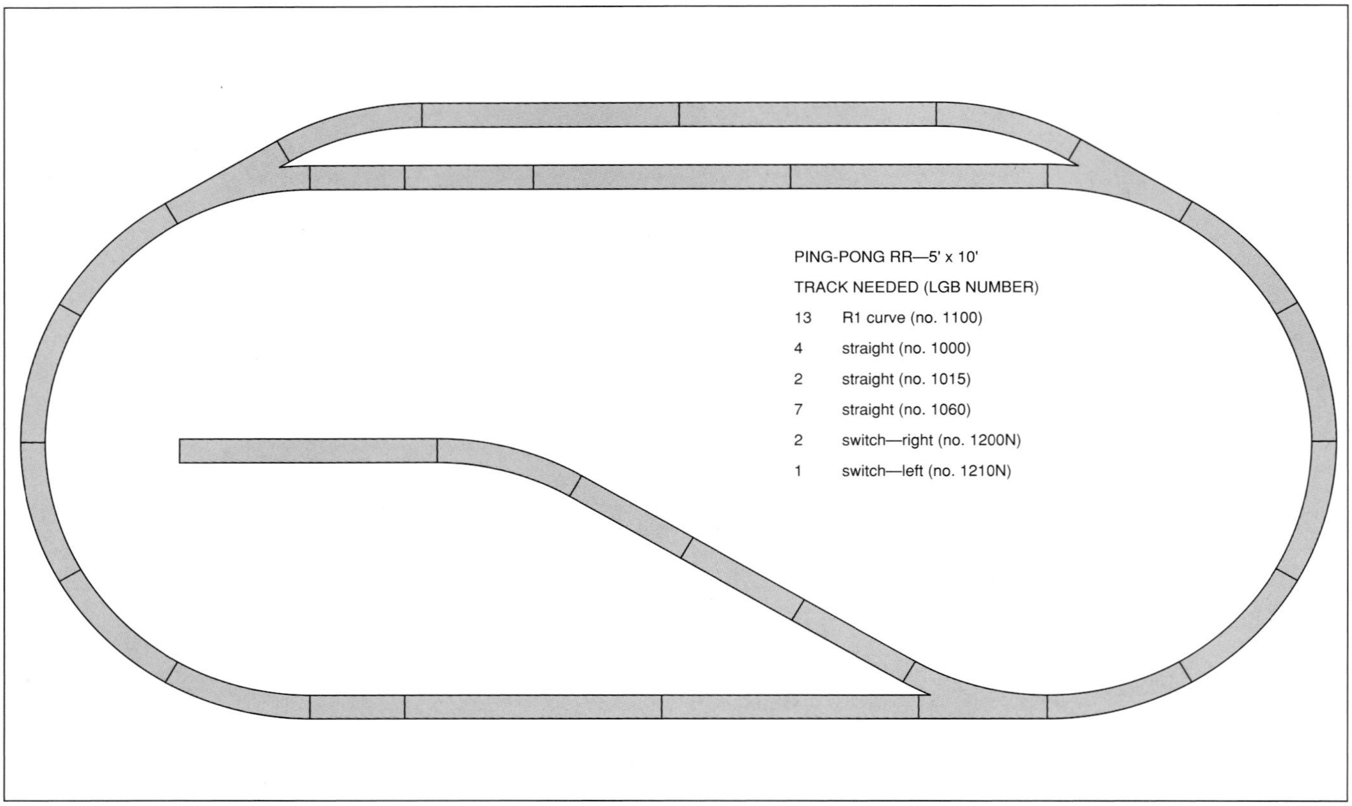

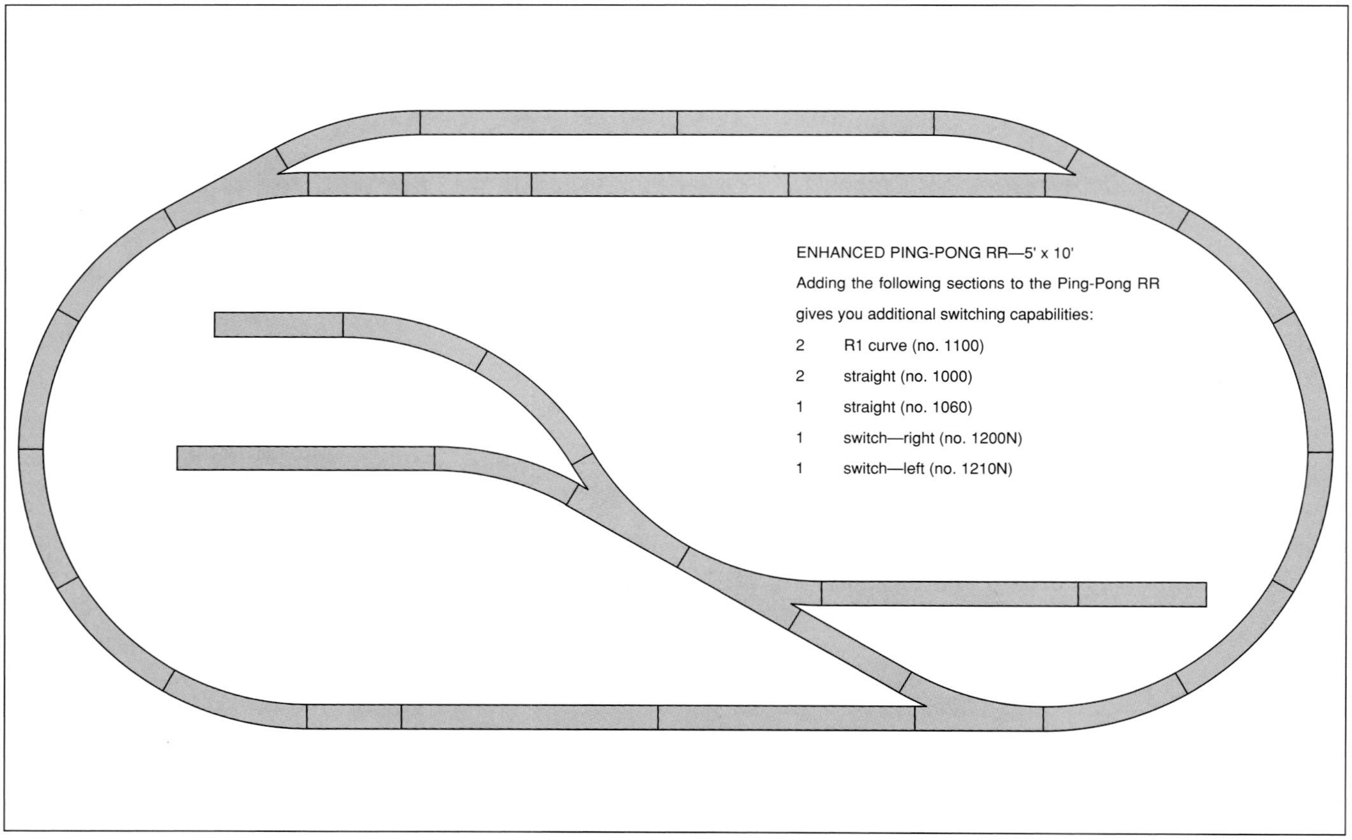

FIG. 2-13. The Ping-Pong Railroad (above) and the Enhanced Ping-Pong Railroad (below).

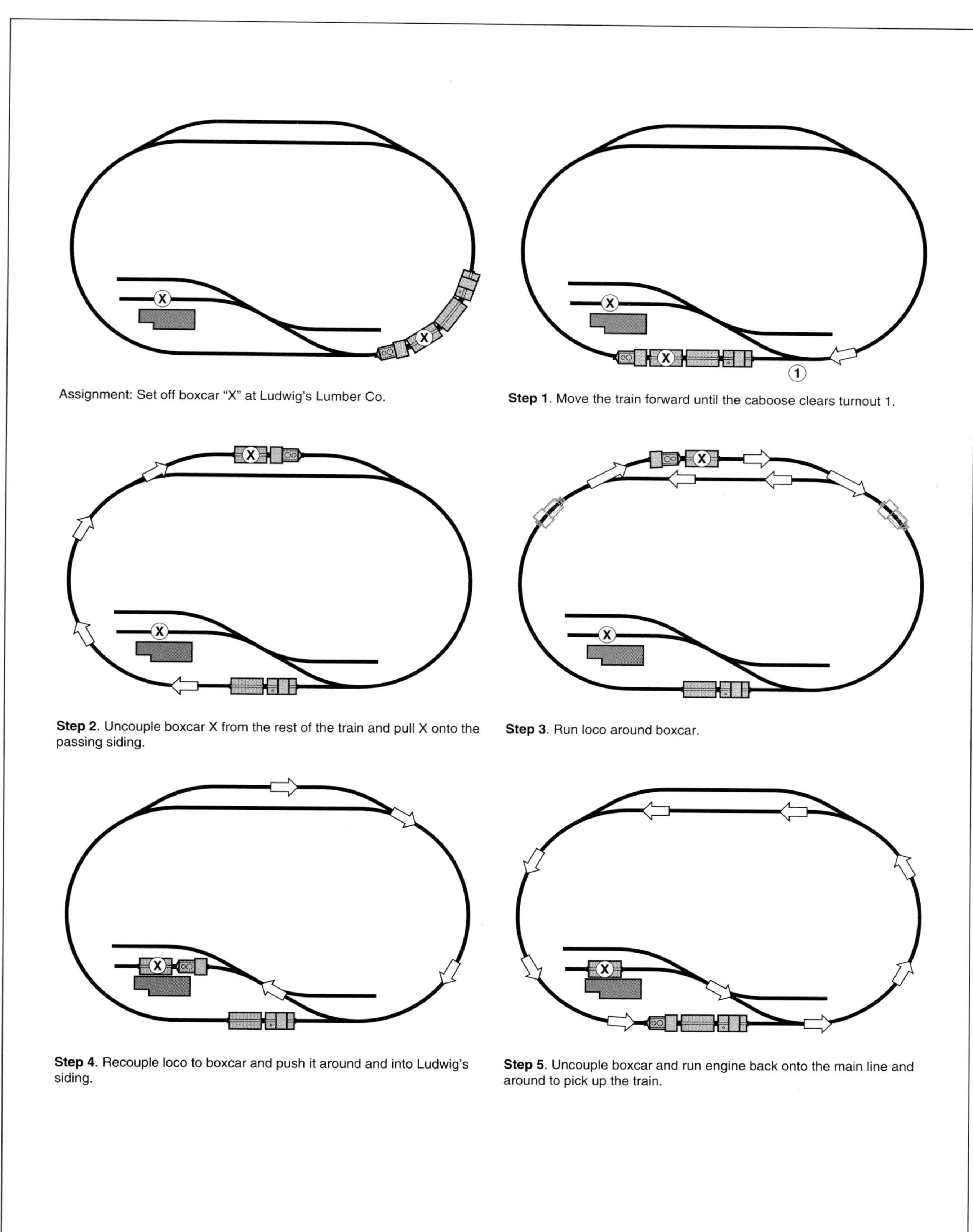

FIG. 2-14. Solving a switching problem like this one on the Enhanced Ping-Pong Railroad can be a lot of fun.

FIG. 2-15. Coauthor Russ Larson reads a train storybook to grandson Aaron. Many good children's books are available with train themes. This is a good way to stimulate the child's imagination. Photo by Barb Larson.

Could is available today, along with such popular new books as *The Polar Express.* And some of the Thomas the Tank Engine books, which British children have loved for many years, are offered in the United States by Random House. Check at a children's book store or your public library.

A FUTURE MODEL RAILROADER?

Not all children will fall in love with their trains, but for some it will be their favorite toy. You can encourage their growing interest in trains by buying more track, turnouts, and cars. If a 9 or 10-year-old child seems really interested in trains, help him or her build a small model railroad. It will be a project that you'll both enjoy. You'll not only enjoy building the railroad, but also all the related activities you both can do together, such as visiting the hobby shop, attending shows and conventions, poring over the latest issues of *Model Railroader, Garden Railways,* or *Classic Toy Trains* magazines, watching railroad videos, going out to trackside, or taking a trip on Amtrak. You'll be helping your child get started in the wonderful hobby of model railroading—an interesting, multifaceted leisure-time activity with enough challenges to last a lifetime.

The Shealy family, **figs. 2-16** and **2-17,** is a good example of a family enjoying the hobby together. Dr. Fred Shealy has fond memories of the Lionel and American Flyer trains he enjoyed as a boy. So when his oldest son, Gray, was 5 and showed some interest in trains, Dad went shopping. Fred was impressed with the quality of LGB trains he saw at this local hobby shop, so he bought Gray a starter set.

That purchase caused Fred's daughter, Heather, and youngest son, Wells, to become interested in trains too. So Fred built a 15 x 30-foot L-shaped G scale layout that fills the kids' playhouse.

The layout is a child's dream come true. Over 300 feet of LGB track on two levels carry up to four trains operating simultaneously under automatic control using LGB's EPL system. There are 12 locomotives, 63 cars, 36 buildings, and over 250 figures. There are scenery features, backdrops, and an operating turntable. What more could a youngster want?

The finished layout is just what Fred intended it to be—a fantasy world that he and his children can enjoy together.

FIG. 2-16. *The Shealy children, left to right, Wells, Heather, and Gray, have a G scale layout in their playhouse that Dad enjoys operating too. Photo by Andy Sperandeo.*

FIG. 2-17. Most of the equipment on the Shealys' layout is LGB, both U.S. and European prototype. The layout features lots of details, including over 250 figures. Photo by Andy Sperandeo.

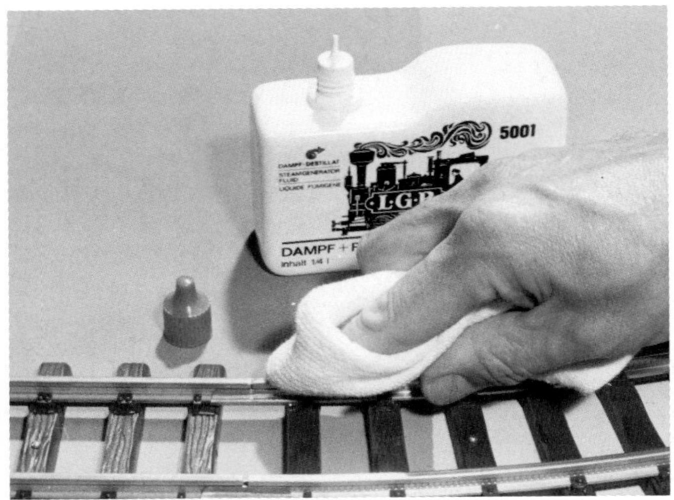

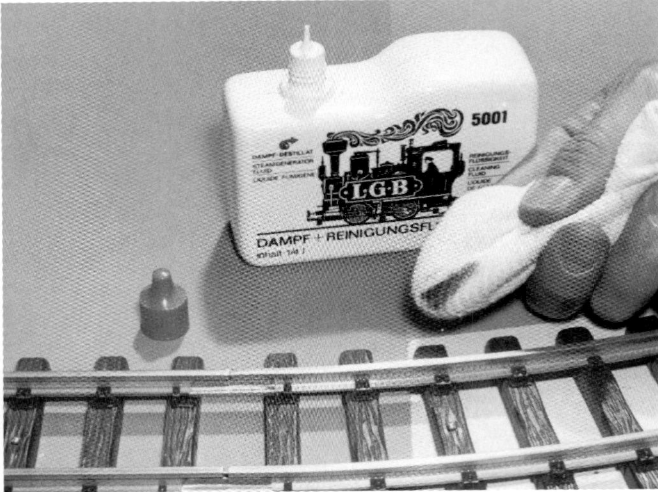

FIG. 2-18. Dirty track is the most common cause of operating problems. Liquid track cleaners work well. Apply the cleaning fluid to a soft cloth and rub the top and inside edge of the rails to remove dirt and oxidation. Photos by Art Schmidt.

MAINTENANCE TIPS

Generally speaking, large scale trains are well made and require very little maintenance. Be sure to read the maintenance information that comes with the train set or locomotive you've purchased.

Dirty track and/or wheels. If you do have any problems with large scale trains, they'll probably involve the locomotives. If a locomotive's operation becomes balky, if it momentarily stops or slows down, the problem is most likely due to dirty track or wheels or both.

There are two ways to clean track: using a track cleaning fluid or using a cleaning pad or block. Several brands of track cleaning fluid are sold at hobby shops. They all seem to work about the same. LGB's liquid smoke can also be used for cleaning track. Apply the fluid to a soft cloth and then wipe it along the top and inside edge of the rail, as shown in **fig. 2-18.**

A track cleaning block that looks something like a big eraser, called Bright Boy, is sold in hobby shops and works fine for cleaning track. LGB also sells its own track cleaning block, which is big enough to clean both rails simultaneously. (See **fig. 2-19.**)

Clean the locomotive's wheels and track pickup wipers with a track cleaning fluid. A cloth works fine to apply the fluid to the wipers. A Q-Tip or similar applicator works well for the wheels. (See **fig. 2-20.**)

Another option is to purchase Kadee's Speedi driver clearer (#843). With this handy gadget you can quickly and thoroughly clean even the grimiest wheels. It's especially helpful if you operate your trains outside, where locomotive wheels get dirty fast. Power is applied to

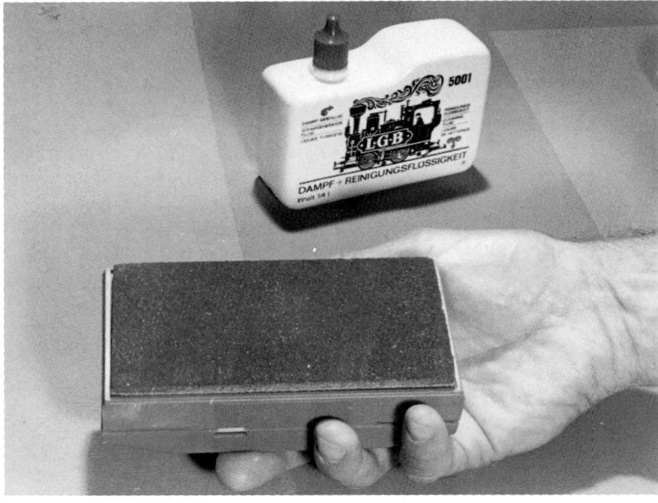

FIG. 2-19. If you operate your trains outdoors, a heavier-duty approach to track cleaning will be required. LGB offers the abrasive block shown, which can be used as is—or fine sandpaper may be attached to it for really dirty track. Sanding blocks sold in hardware stores are just the right width for gauge 1 track. Photos by Art Schmidt.

FIG. 2-20. Next to dirty track, the most common source of trouble is dirty locomotive wheels and pickup shoes. The same cleaner used for track can be used for wheels and pickup shoes too. Apply the cleaner to the wheels and shoes with a Q-Tip and wipe clean with a soft cloth. Photos by Art Schmidt.

the drivers through Speedi's metal bristles, so the wheels turn into the bristles, as shown in **fig. 2-21.**

Lubrication. The cars don't require any lubrication. For the locomotives, follow the manufacturer's guidelines for frequency and the type of oil or grease to use for gears and metal-to-metal surfaces like steam locomotive valve gear, crank pins, and drive rods. Be sure the oils and greases you use are plastic-compatible.

Brushes. Motor brushes eventually wear out and need to be replaced, but this will take years under normal use. The two brushes carry the electric current to the motor's armature. If the brushes are not making proper contact with the armature, the motor will run erratically or not at all. Follow the manufacturer's instructions for brush replacement or take the locomotive to your hobby shop for repair.

Other problems. Locomotive light bulbs will eventually burn out and need to be replaced. After long use, traction tires and pickup shoes will wear out.

Unless the equipment is abused, you should have very little maintenance—one of the big advantages of these big trains.

FIG. 2-21. Kadee makes this handy locomotive driver cleaner. The Speedi driver cleaner is connected to the DC output of your power pack. The wire brush bristles transfer electrical power to the wheels, turning them to speed the cleaning process. Photo by Art Schmidt.

CHAPTER THREE

Ways for Adults to Enjoy Large Scale

FIG. 3-1. Colorado & Southern no. 22 eases away from the Jefferson, Colorado, depot in this dramatic G scale night scene by Joe Crea. This is a fine example of the realism that can be attained with an indoor large scale layout. He scratchbuilt the depot and included interior details. The snow was simulated by plaster sprinkled onto the scene with a flour sifter. Photo by Joe Crea.

by Russ Larson

In this chapter we'll show you the three primary ways adults enjoy large scale trains as a hobby:

1. You can build an indoor empire, just as model railroaders do in the smaller scales.
2. You can even take these rugged trains outside and build a garden railway.
3. Or you may find a great deal of satisfaction in collecting and displaying large scale trains.

And there's absolutely nothing preventing you from enjoying these versatile trains in all three ways—or in any other manner that keeps you satisfied!

LARGE SCALE TRAINS INDOORS

In the previous chapter we looked at ways for children to enjoy large scale trains. Sure, a train board with some structures and scenery can serve as a model railroad, but an adult model railroader usually takes the illusion a few steps further along by developing a concept for his railroad.

What is the concept? It's the plan for the railroad that defines its purpose and geographical setting and sets the era.

As much as is practical, a model railroader working in large scale will have models of the same or nearly the same scale. If it's a standard gauge layout, all the railroad equipment will be 1:32 proportion, as will the structures and figures.

If it's a narrow gauge layout, all the locomotives and cars will be 1:22.5 proportion, as will the structures and figures. Some modelers may compromise and use the slightly smaller 1:24 (1/2" scale) structures, vehicles, and accessories that are available from dealers in the field of dollhouse miniatures.

A model railroader also tries to keep all elements in agreement with the time period being modeled. If the concept describes the railroad as a 1920s era Colorado narrow gauge railroad serving mining towns, you shouldn't see any diesel locomotives or any cars or trucks from a more modern time.

Obviously, there are many other details that need to be in sync with the times, such as building architecture, clothing styles, street lights, advertising billboards, signs, and posters. Getting all these elements reasonably accurate can become a learning experience for the model railroader.

GARDEN RAILROADING

Garden railroading is probably the fastest-growing aspect of the model train hobby today. In Chapters 6 and 7 we'll examine garden railroading in more depth. For now, though, here's a brief overview of this fascinating aspect of the hobby.

Garden railroading is the art of combining a model railroad and a beautiful garden to create a railway-like atmosphere. The difference between a traditional indoor layout and a garden railway is the difference between realism and reality.

Indoors, the goal is to create the illusion of reality through the use of artificial material. For example, mountains are made of plaster and rivers of plastic casting resin. Outdoors, though, you deal with real life. Mountains are made of dirt and rock and rivers are made using real water.

This can be both a blessing and a curse. Track gets washed out, branches fall on the track, flowers grow across the track, etc. But when you compare these nuisances to the joy of having a railroad at your doorstep that is constantly growing and changing with the seasons, the weather, and even the time of day, this seems a small price to pay. Some garden railroaders even consider the nuisances to be part of the fun!

Gardening is a fascinating aspect of the hobby. Railway gardening has become a sub-hobby in its own right. And in fact, it is the garden that often draws entire families into the hobby.

You don't have to know anything about gardening to get started. Many beautiful garden railways have been created by people who claim they are not gardeners. You can learn what you need to know by reading gardening magazines and books and by visiting garden centers and gardens in your area.

If you think you might be interested in garden railroading, join a local garden railway society. Get out and visit local garden railroaders. Meet people and have fun. That's what garden railroading is all about!

COLLECTING

Another aspect of the hobby is collecting. What makes a toy or model a collectible is a subject for much discussion. Age, limited production, as well as mistakes in

FIG. 3-2. You can also create a realistic outdoor garden railway in G scale. Dean and Sandy Lowe operate Colorado & Southern equipment on their beautiful Gn3 layout located behind their California home. Dean weathered all his rolling stock and added extra details to his locomotives. The Lowes have selected ground cover, flowers, and trees that blend well together. Photo by Dean Lowe.

FIG. 3-3. This beautifully displayed large scale collection of John Gummo includes No. 1 scale models of F3 diesels in the foreground and steam-era European prototype passenger cars in the wall display cases. Photo by Chris Becker.

production are all factors in a model's attractiveness to collectors.

Clearly, some of the exquisitely detailed large scale models offered by Aster, Eastern Railways, Marketing Corporation of America, Märklin, and others are intended to appeal to collectors. No. 1 and G scale models offered by these firms can run $2000 to $5000 or more.

To become a collector of large scale trains, first and foremost you must have the desire to form a collection with some theme. For example, you might want to have one example of everything made by a certain manufacturer. There are quite a few collectors of LGB equipment. Other people collect those pieces that they find appealing personally. If you have a favorite prototype railroad, for instance, you could collect models of its equipment.

Once you know what you're after, the chase is on. Collectors go to great lengths to get the models they want to complete their collection. They attend auctions and shows, they study classified ads in magazines, they haggle with collector friends. It's an exciting sport for those with the knowledge and money to participate.

CHAPTER FOUR

Building an Indoor Layout

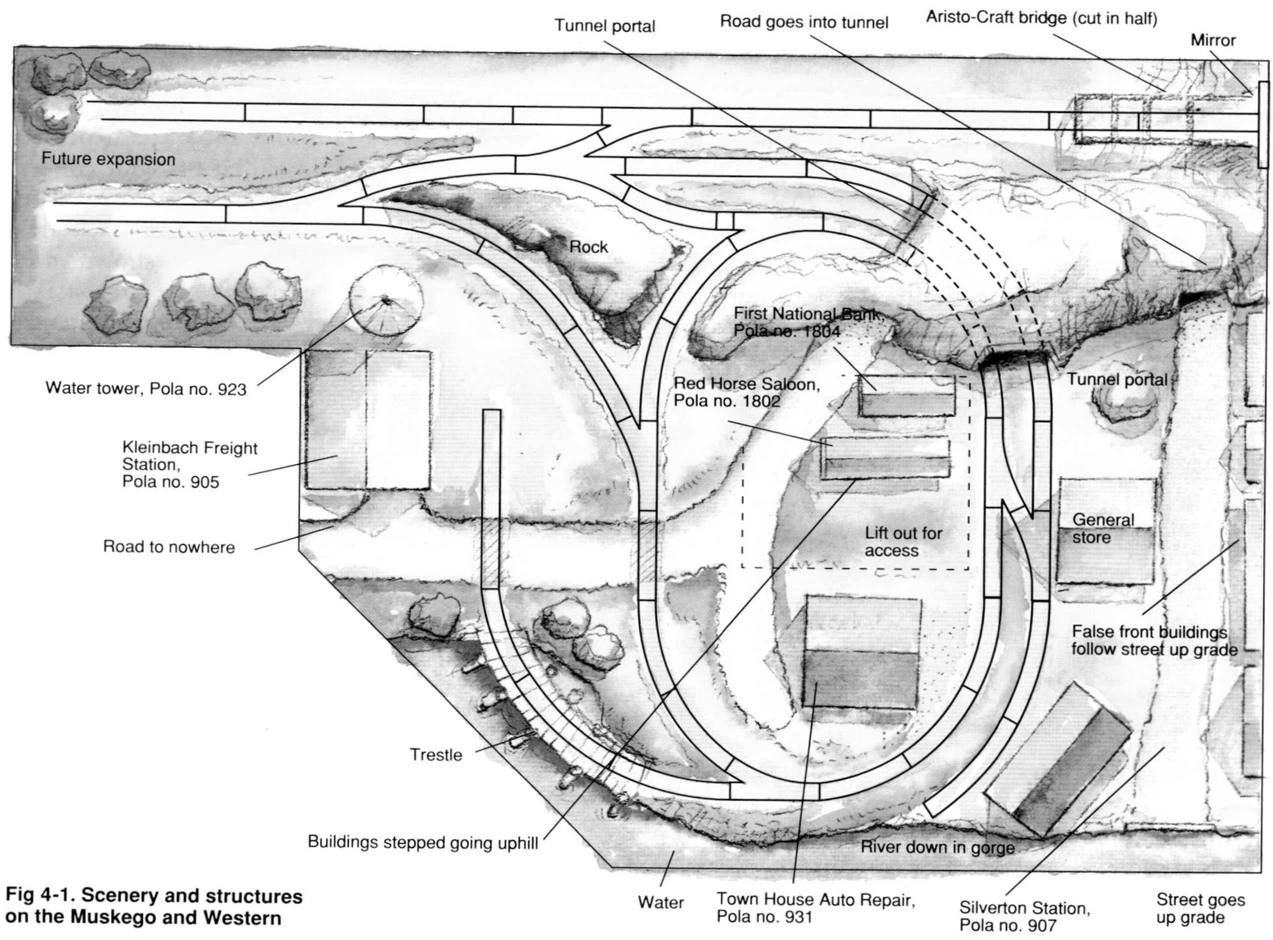

FIG. 4-1. Artist's rendering of the completed Muskego & Western. The steps presented throughout the chapter will help you construct this layout or one that you design.

by Russ Larson

Model railroading is a sophisticated hobby—one with enough challenges to provide a lifetime of intellectually stimulating enjoyment. In building a layout you'll discover how multifaceted model railroading is. It involves railroading, of course, and model building, along with woodworking, electrical and mechanical engineering, art, photography, geography, geology, architecture, and history. The satisfaction in this hobby comes from learning new skills and applying them to the task at hand.

The decision to build a model railroad, whether inside or outside, is a commitment—a commitment of money and, most importantly, of your precious leisure time. A typical model railroad hobbyist spends about ten hours a week enjoying the hobby. It can take years to get a layout to the "finished" stage. Actually, a model railroad is never really finished. There will always be areas you'll want to change as your

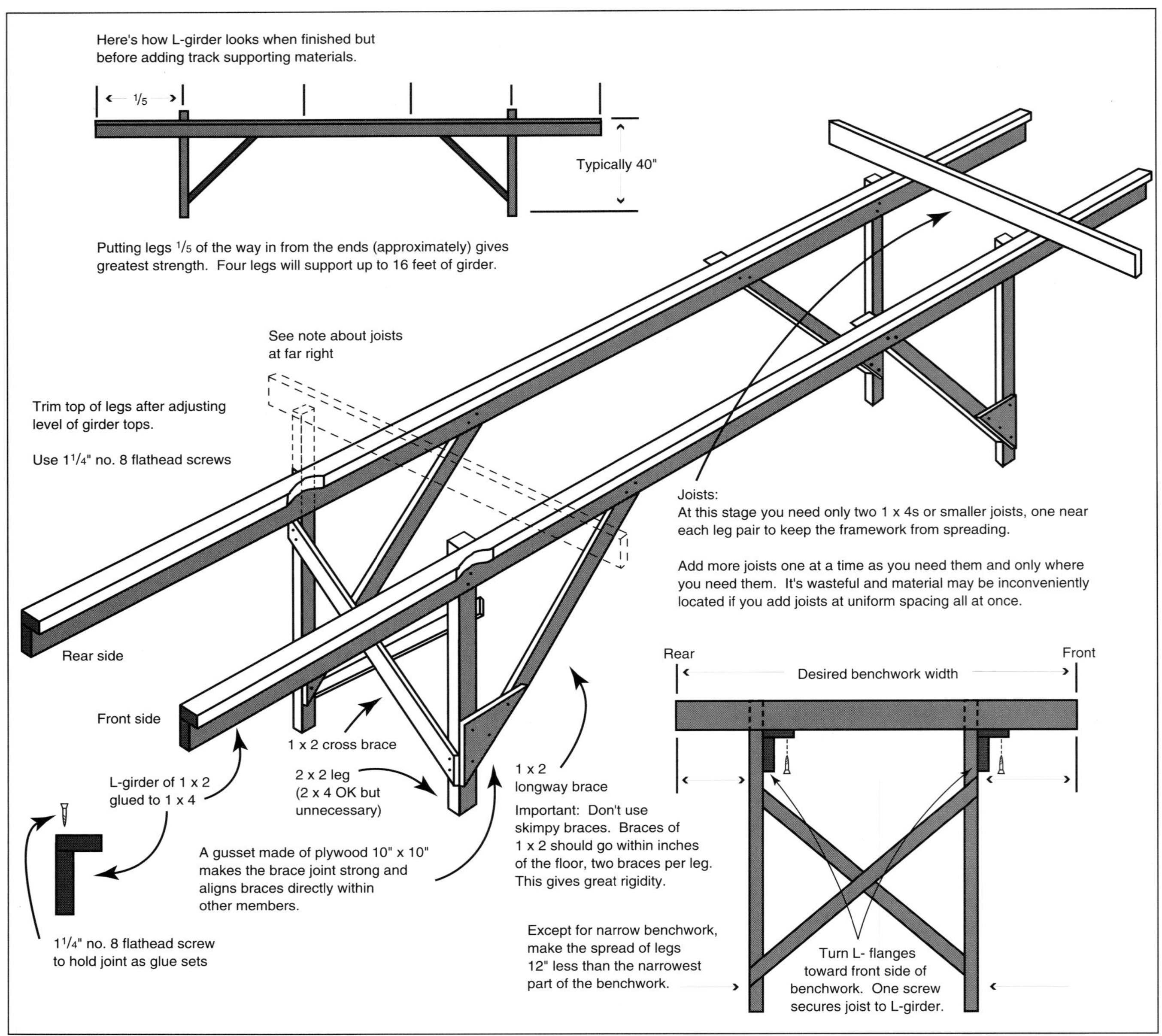

FIG. 4-4. L-girder framework relies for its sturdiness on engineering design rather than brute strength of material. The benchwork is light but strong.

BENCHWORK

In model railroad terminology, benchwork is the supporting structure for the roadbed and track. There are many ways to build benchwork. A very basic layout would be a sheet of plywood laid on a couple of sawhorses. In this example the sawhorses are the benchwork.

The benchwork used for the Muskego & Western, shown in the accompanying illustration, is called L-girder. (See **fig. 4-4.**) It's a method that was developed in the 1960s by the late Linn Westcott, long-time editor of *Model Railroader* magazine. It quickly became the most popular benchwork system because it's strong, simple to build by amateur carpenters (like me), and can be changed easily. Linn wrote a book titled *How to Build Model Railroad Benchwork,* which includes a detailed description of L-girder benchwork.

Tools required. The assembly is to be screwed together, so you'll need a 3/8" variable-speed, reversible electric drill with screwdriver bits. You'll need a saber saw to cut the wood pieces to size and lots of C-clamps (a minimum of a half dozen) to hold pieces temporarily while you screw them together. You'll also want a square and a level to make sure that your assembled benchwork is reasonably square and level.

Work safely. Make sure your power tools are plugged into grounded outlets. Always wear safety glasses when using power

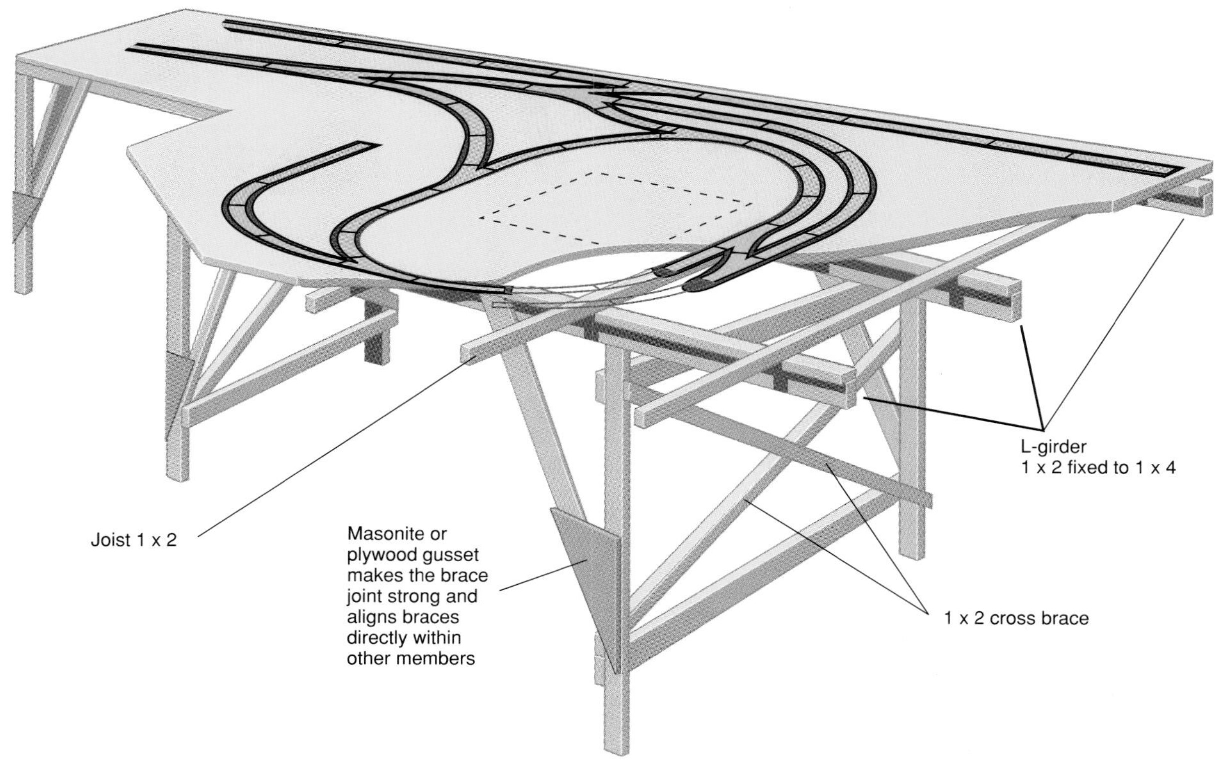

FIG. 4-5. Benchwork for the Muskego & Western was built using easy-to-build L-girder framework.

tools and a dust mask when cutting wood. Of course, watch where your hands are in relation to the power tools at all times. You can seriously injure yourself with a saber saw if you're careless.

Making L-girders. Begin construction by making the L-girders themselves from 1 x 4s and 1 x 2s. (See **fig. 4-5.**) A 1 x 4 is used for the long leg of the L and a 1 x 2 for the short leg. Assemble the two pieces, using yellow carpenter's glue. Use screws to hold the pieces tightly together until the glue sets. You could back the screws out after the glue sets and reuse them, but most modelers don't bother. Many modelers now use drywall screws because you don't need to first drill a pilot hole.

Leg assemblies. Next, make the leg assemblies from 2 x 2s and 1 x 2s. In addition to the screws, I always apply glue to all joints.

Putting it all together. I mounted one L-girder directly to the wall and the other two to leg assemblies as shown. The leg assemblies and the two L-girders make a free-standing table. When this had been assembled following the sequence shown, I fastened 1 x 2 joists in place, thus tying the whole assembly together.

I mounted plywood directly to the joists because I wanted the track level. On a small layout like this you don't have enough track length to vary the grade much.

Risers. On larger layouts you may want to gradually raise and lower the track for reasons of track design and to achieve a more realistic look. The beauty of L-girder benchwork is that you can do that easily by installing risers to the joists. The risers can be adjusted to give you a nice gradual grade. Make

FIG. 4-6 (left). After the joists are fastened in place, they are cut to length. FIG. 4-7 (right). The author tests to make certain all areas are accessible from the access opening (indicated by dotted lines in fig. 4-5).

sure the change in grade is gradual and that your grades do not exceed 3 percent (a 3" change in elevation in 100"). See Chapter 10 for information on calculating grades.

TRACKLAYING

Roadbed. Track can be fastened directly to the wood subroadbed, and that's what I'd recommend for a first small layout. Using a cork roadbed between the wood and the track helps deaden the sound of the train and raises the track up a little from the surrounding terrain, which is prototypical.

When I was building this indoor G scale layout, no commercial cork strips were offered for G scale, so I cut my own. Large hardware stores sell 1/8" cork in bulk. They offer 3- and 4-foot widths and will cut it to whatever length you want.

LGB track ties are 3½" long, so I cut the cork in 4" strips, as shown in **fig. 4-9.** For curves, I found it's easier to use two strips of 2" wide cork rather than one 4" wide strip.

When used under straight track, the cork doesn't require any special fastening. The screws or nails that hold the track will hold the cork as well. However, on curves I suggest putting the track temporarily in position and marking the center line. Remove the track and apply white

FIG. 4-8. Temporarily assemble the track on the completed benchwork, then mark the position on the plywood.

Step 1.

Step 2.

Step 3.

FIG. 4-9. Installing cork roadbed. Step 1: Cut cork in 4" strips or two strips of 2" width. Step 2: Remove the temporarily assembled track and apply glue to the marked roadbed area. Step 3: Install roadbed using the marks on the plywood as your guide. Staple to secure in place.

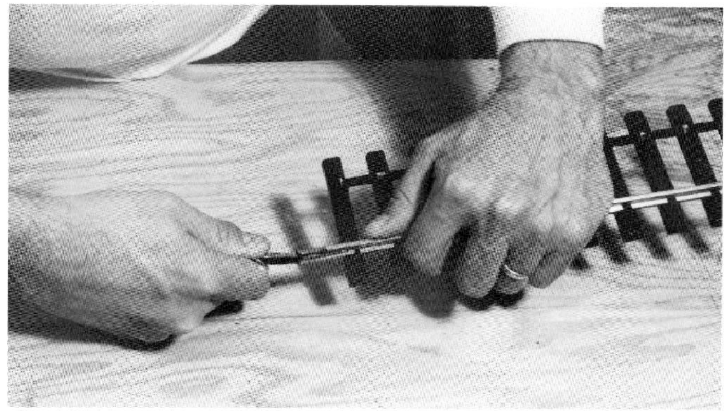

Step 1.

Step 2.

Step 3.

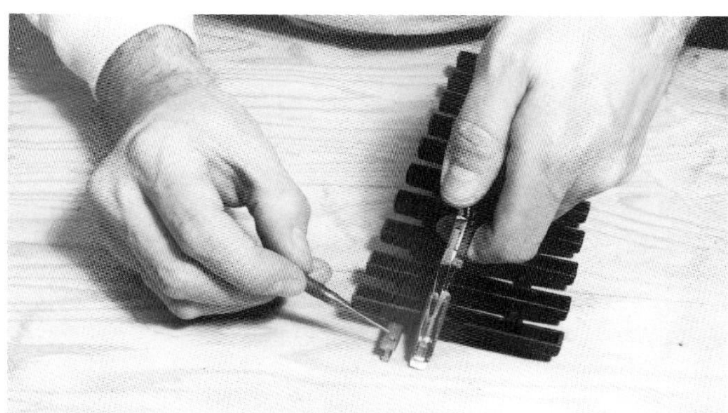

Step 4.

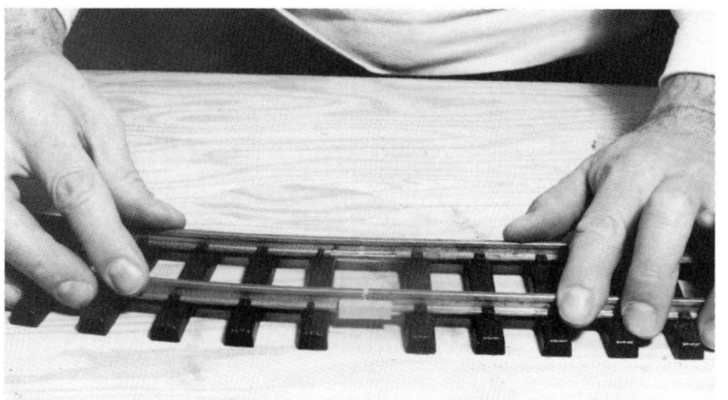

Step 5.

FIG. 4-10. Installing insulated rail joiners. Step 1: Grasp the joiner with a small flat-nosed pliers. Step 2: Rotate the joiner left and right until it breaks free. Step 3: This back-and-forth motion will twist the joiner and make it unusable. Step 4: This photo shows why the joiners are difficult to remove. The joiners are crimped to the rail and one spot is punched into the rail. Step 5: Slide the insulated joiner on one rail and join the sections together.

glue to the area where the roadbed will be installed. (See **fig. 4-9,** step 2.) Install the 2" wide cork strips on each side of the center line and staple in place with a lightweight staple gun. (See **fig. 4-9,** step 3.) Wherever the cork bulges due to the curvature, remove V-shaped slices with a hobby knife.

Insulated rail joiners. You'll note that the plan, **fig. 4-2,** shows locations of insulated rail joiners. These plastic joiners connect the track pieces physically but insulate adjoining pieces electrically. In the section on wiring, I'll explain why they are necessary. To install these insulated joiners, you have to twist off the metal joiners. (See **fig. 4-10.**)

Track mounting. Gauge 1 track can be fastened with either screws or nails. Screws have a more positive grip into the wood than nails. The disadvantage is that the screw heads are relatively large and unsightly. However, if they are painted dark brown or black, they are not too noticeable.

No. 3 x ½" screws are ideal if you're mounting track directly to plywood. If you're using cork subroadbed to deaden sound, then you'll have to go to ¾" long screws. I couldn't find this length in no. 3 size, so I had to go to the larger no. 4. No. 4s can be threaded into the holes predrilled in LGB track. For extra holes in the track and for holes in turnouts that don't come predrilled, use a 5/64" bit.

LGB turnouts have mounting holes on the point end and on the

Step 1.

Step 2.

Step 3.

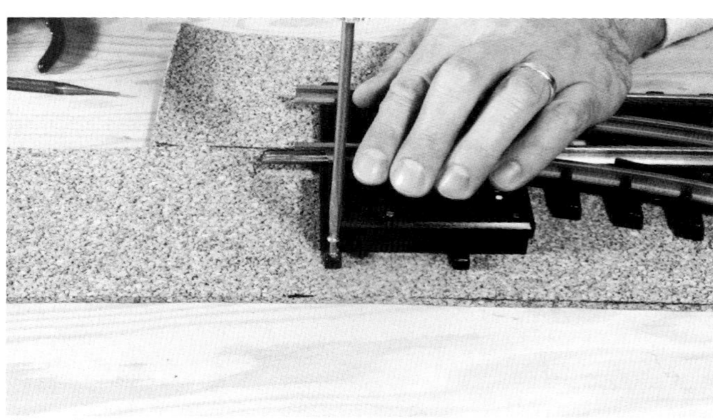

Step 4.

FIG. 4-11. Mounting Track. Step 1: Use 1" nails to fasten the track to the roadbed and plywood. Step 2: A nail punch will prevent you from damaging the ties or rails with the hammer. Step 3: LGB turnouts have molded-in mounting holes. Drilling pilot holes also makes it easier to drive a nail or screw into the cork roadbed and plywood. Step 4: A no. 4 screw with a dab of yellow glue on the tip will ensure that the track stays in place.

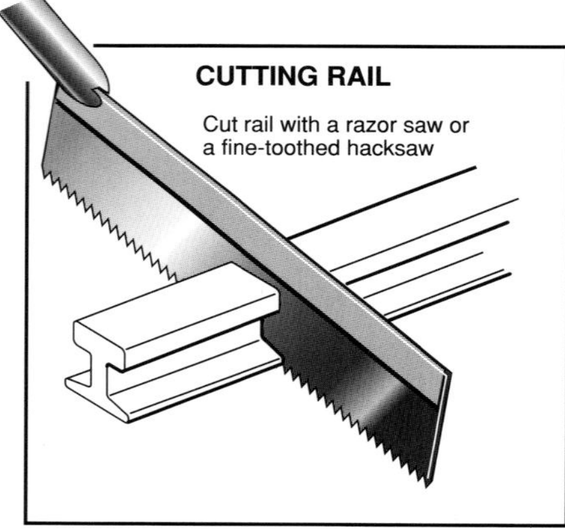

FIG. 4-12 Cutting rail.

outer edge of the electric switch machines. (See **fig. 4-11.**) The no. 4 screws work in these turnout holes as well.

Small wire nails can also be used to mount the track. If you're mounting directly to plywood, use ¾" nails. If you're using cork roadbed, use 1" nails. The tiny heads of wire nails are almost invisible. Drilling no. 61 pilot holes makes it easier to drive home the small nails. To ensure that the nails will hold the track in place, dab a little yellow glue on the tips of the nails.

Cutting rail. There are a couple of places on the layout where you have to cut a piece of track to make it fit. This can be easily done with a razor saw with a sharp blade. (See **fig. 4-12.**)

Test run. After the track is mounted, connect some temporary track feeders and try running several locomotives over the layout. Take the time to make sure that everything works smoothly before you apply the ballast—because once the ballast is fixed in place, it'll be much more difficult to make changes.

BALLASTING

Real railroads use crushed rock for ballast that varies in size between 1" and 3" in diameter. That means G scale ballast should range roughly between 1⁄32" and ⅛" in diameter. Crushed stone graded to the proper size for each scale is available in hobby shops. When I began working in G, ballast was not offered. A friend suggested chicken grit, which is crushed granite. I found that the finer grit intended for young chickens is just the right size. It looks good and it's inexpensive.

Ballasting procedure: A paper or plastic cup makes a good ballast dispenser. (See **fig. 4-13.**) Simply pour the ballast between the rails and on each side. Be sure to pour enough so that the ballast comes up to the top of the ties. Next level the ballast, using a brush. A large artist's or small paint brush works fine.

Apply ballast sparingly under the

Step 1.

Step 2.

Step 3.

Step 4.

FIG. 4-13. Step 1: Pour ballast between the rails on each side. Next, level the ballast with a small paintbrush. Step 2: Clear stones off the top of the ties and the base of the rails using a small, stiff artist's brush. Step 3: Spray the ballast with water containing a few drops of detergent. Step 4: Fix the ballast by applying diluted white glue to the wet ballast using an ear syringe.

turnout points so that the point movement isn't obstructed. Make sure no ballast gets into the turnout guard rails or the groove where the turnout throw rod travels.

Take your time when applying ballast, as the shape of the ballast will affect the looks of your railroad. Use a small, stiff artist's brush to clear stones off the tops of the ties and from the base of the rails.

G scale ballast is large enough that it doesn't really have to be glued in place. However, I would recommend it. Otherwise, you may mess up the shape of the ballast while working on the layout, or your nicely shaped ballast could be rearranged by a derailment. Having the ballast fixed in place will make it easier to cover when doing scenery and will allow you to paint the ballast or track later with an airbrush.

Fixing ballast. The ballast can be fixed in place with either diluted white glue or matte medium. I used a 1:1 mix of white glue and water with a few drops of liquid detergent added. A much more watery mix works for smaller scales, but I found that these "large" stones need a stronger glue content to hold them in place.

When you have the ballast arranged the way you want it, fill a spray bottle with water and add a few drops of detergent. A plant spray bottle works well for this. Spray the ballast with water. The detergent makes the water spread out and get between all the stones, ensuring that the white glue mix will get there too.

After the stone is wet, apply the white glue-water mix liberally. For smaller scales we recommend using an eyedropper, but for the quantity required for G scale I've found an ear syringe works best. Apply the mix only to the ballast. Try to avoid getting glue on the ties and rail. This will make cleanup easier. Rinse the ear syringe with warm water after each use or it will become hopelessly clogged and have to be thrown away.

Spray the ballast with "wet" water again after applying the glue. This helps spread the glue evenly and also washes off any glue that was splashed on the ties. After the white glue mix dries, the ballast will be bonded together rock-hard, yet still look loose. It can take up to two days for the glue to dry in areas where the ballast is deep.

WIRING

Cab control is a popular method of wiring a layout so that two or more people can run trains. It's described in Chapter 10. True cab control doesn't really make sense on a layout this small. Our little oval is

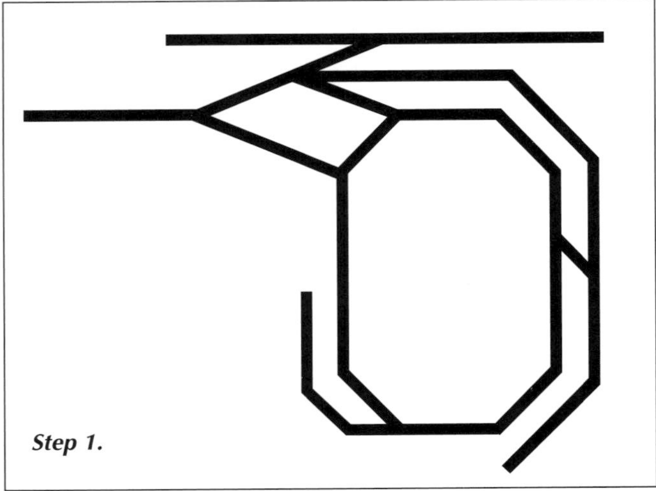

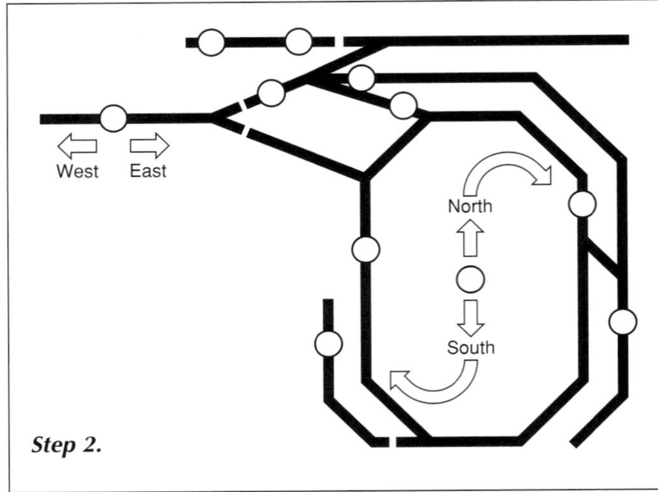

FIG. 4-14. Constructing the control panel. Step 1: After the first coat of white or yellow paint on the Masonite panel board has dried, draw your track plan on the panel. Then place thin strips of masking tape over the drawing and paint again with a darker color. Step 2: When the paint dries, peel off the tape, drill holes for the switches, and label the panel. Step 3: Once the switches are mounted and wired, you're ready to run trains.

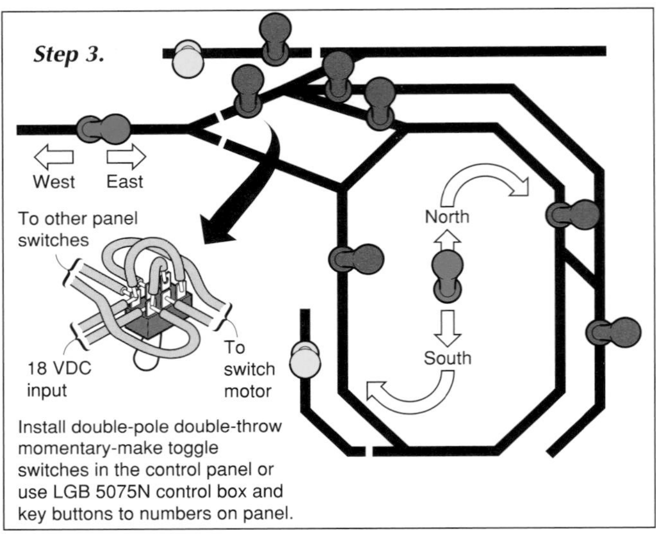

only about 16 feet in circumference. In order to have a practical cab control system, each block has to be at least as long as your longest train (a small freight consisting of engine, two cars, and a caboose is about 5 feet long).

So theoretically you could split this oval into three blocks (the minimum to run two trains), but the blocks would be too short for practical operation. For a large scale layout you'll want blocks that are a minimum of 30 feet long.

Train control. I suggest wiring this small layout for one-train operation. I would suggest that at least one siding have an insulated rail joiner installed in one rail and power be supplied via a single-pole, single-throw on-off switch. This enables you to "park" one engine in the siding while you operate another one on the layout. The **fig. 4-2** wiring plan shows two sidings controlled by an on-off switch to give you a little operating variety.

Reverse loop. The wiring of this little layout is somewhat complicated by a reverse loop. Whenever the track arrangement allows a train to reverse direction and reenter a section of track going in the opposite direction, special wiring is required. More detailed information on reverse loop wiring can be found in Chapter 10. The illustration (**fig. 4-2**) shows you what to do.

Turnout control. Turnout points are thrown either with solenoids or motors. LGB turnouts are thrown with motors controlled by momentary-make, double-pole, double-throw (DPDT) switches. You can buy switches like this with a current rating of at least 1 amp at electronic supply stores and wire them as shown in **fig. 4-14,** step 3. I like toggle-type switches because they can be mounted in your control panel schematic at the position corresponding to the turnout that they control.

LGB also sells a panel of switches for turnout control (5075N), which come mounted in a box. If you use the LGB switches, number them and key the numbers to the turnout locations on the panel.

The control panel. The switches that control the power to the sidings and the switches for reverse loop control are handiest to use if mounted on a control panel. The switches that control the turnouts can also be mounted on this panel.

It's easy to make a control panel from a sheet of Masonite mounted in a 1 x 1 frame as shown in **fig. 4-14.**

Begin by spraying the panel white or yellow. Then draw a schematic of your track plan on the panel. Place thin masking tape over the drawing. Spray the panel again in the final color desired. After the paint has dried, peel off the tape. Finally, drill holes for your switches and mount them. Complete the wiring, and you're ready to run your trains.

SCENERY AND STRUCTURES

Scenery is easy to build, and it really transforms a "train board" into a full-fledged model railroad. Scenery gives a layout its personality. It is the vertical dimension of the model railroad.

The looks of even a small layout like this will change dramatically when scenery and structures are added. My plans for the layout included a rocky ridge that would serve to block the view between the town scene and the line that crosses the bridge that ends in the "mirror trick." (See **fig. 4-1.**)

That rock outcropping gives us a natural reason to bring the street scene upgrade. Placing the buildings at different elevations and having the street and sidewalk going uphill adds a lot of interest.

Having a rock outcropping also means that the railroad will have to tunnel through it. A tunnel is a scenic highlight that many model railroaders want to include on their layouts.

Another rock outcropping in the wye and a trestle over a creek on the industrial spur complete the major scenic features on this small layout.

You can spend many enjoyable hours on scenery for a small layout like this. Unfortunately, many people never experience these facets of the hobby because they are afraid to try them. They think you have to be an artist. By following proven scenery-building techniques, anyone can build good-looking scenery. And if painting backdrops seems beyond your artistic reach, printed ones are available.

Scenery and structures go together. In fact, some people consider structures to be a part of the scenery. So you need to plan scenic highlights and structure placement at the same time.

Backdrops. Backdrops really finish the look of scenery. Even simple ones that consist of just blue sky with some clouds help a lot. Those that contain scenes that blend with the foreground can be dynamite.

Untempered Masonite is a good backdrop material. It has a good surface for painting, and you can bend it to form free-flowing curves. If you're going with a plain blue sky backdrop, paint it before you build the foreground scenery.

Scenery forms. Model railroad scenery is commonly made of a thin shell of plaster-soaked paper towels or plaster-impregnated gauze. We need some type of form in the approximate shape of the hills and mountains we want to model to support the plaster-soaked towels until the plaster sets.

A simple scenery form can be made by crumpling up newspapers and taping them in place. Many people find this approach a little crude and prefer to make forms using cardboard strips stapled and glued in place with a hot glue gun.

Hardshell. Hardshell scenery is made by soaking strips of paper toweling (the tough type intended for use in dispensers is best) in soupy plaster and draping them over the scenery forms as shown in **fig. 4-15.**

Any type of plaster will work. Hobby shops sell small bags for this purpose. If you're doing a lot of hardshell, you can buy 50-pound bags at building supply dealers. A particularly strong type of plaster is Hydrocal. If you can't find it, molding plaster is almost as strong and takes color stains better.

The procedure for making hardshell scenery is easy. You'll need a plastic mixing bowl. First pour 1 cup of water into the mixing bowl and add plaster until you have a mix that's like pancake batter (about 2 cups of plaster should do).

Cut the paper towels into strips about 2" wide. Take a strip of toweling and work it into the plaster until it's thoroughly soaked. Then drape it over your supporting structure. Overlap the strips until you have the area covered.

After the plaster sets, wet the surface and then brush on extra plaster to smooth out the rough edges between towel strips.

Plaster dries out the skin, and some people are allergic to it. Wear rubber gloves if this is a problem for you.

Rock castings. Rock strata can be carved into plaster as it's setting, but the most realistic rockwork is cast from rubber molds made from real rock. These molds are sold in hobby shops, or you can make your own.

There are two methods for making rock casting, wet and dry. With the wet method, you plop the mold full of plaster on the hardshell as the plaster is beginning to set. You let it harden in place and then pull off the rubber mold. With the dry method, you simply let the casting harden in the mold, remove it, and fit it in place on the layout. Finally, you trowel plaster into the gaps between castings.

Stain exposed rock surfaces with washes of acrylic paint to give them a realistic color.

Texturing. Hobby shops sell several brands of ground foam. Each brand has a range of colors and grades of coarseness. Begin the texturing process by painting a small area of hardshell with a ground color latex paint. While the paint is still wet, sprinkle on ground foam. A spray application of a mixture of matte medium and water will fix any loose foam in place.

Other materials that can be used to texture surfacing realistically include real dirt, sand, and decomposed granite.

Trees and bushes. Many types of trees are commercially offered for sale, and many articles have been

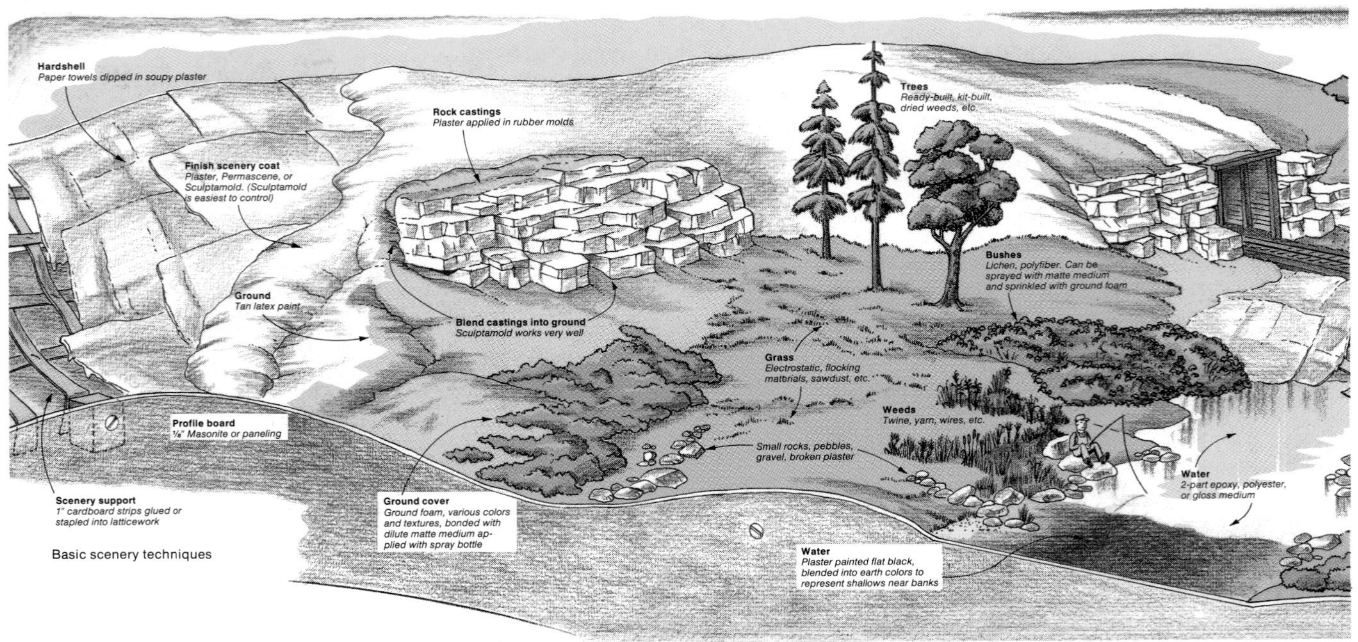

FIG. 4-15. The structure of scenery, from cardboard scenery forms at left to highly detailed areas at right.

written describing ways to make your own. Large scale modeling requires at least some large trees. You can model bushes quite effectively using clumps of lichen, a type of moss that stays "fresh" for years when processed.

Buildings. Many buildings in the style of the Old West are available for large scale. For a Gn3 layout you have a nice selection of Pola plastic kits, which are easy to assemble, need no painting, and can be used indoors or out. I've suggested six Pola buildings that would fit in nicely on the Muskego & Western. (See **fig. 4-1.**) There are also a number of smaller manufacturers who offer plastic and wood kits that would work well also.

There's also a whole line of structures and windows, doors, and detail parts offered for the ½" scale dollhouse miniatures hobby. These parts are handy if you choose to scratchbuild structures working from your own designs or from plans published in magazines and books.

False fronts and mirrors. Because structures take up a lot of square footage, and because you usually don't have that much room on an indoor large scale layout, you need to use every trick you can think of to simulate more buildings than you have room for.

Just modeling the fronts of buildings and placing them along a wall is one easy way to get extra structures on the layout. You can buy kits and just use the fronts, but that's an expensive route to travel. Try buying window and door castings and building your own fronts from plans.

Mirrors can be used effectively to make a small layout look bigger. They must be placed carefully so visitors don't see themselves in the mirror. One trick I used was to cut a bridge in half and butt it up against a mirror, as shown in **fig. 4-1.** Experiment and you'll find other mirror tricks that work. Front-surface mirrors are the most effective for this purpose, but any mirror can be used.

Detailing. After you have the structures and scenery finished to your liking, you can spend many enjoyable hours adding details. You can include details in any scene to make it come to life. There are cars, trucks, animals, and, of course, people. How all the details are finished and positioned can really make a difference in the authenticity of your layout.

It's fun to place figures of people and animals in scenes that tell a story. Why is the crowd gathered around the man lying flat on his back in the middle of the street? Did he have a heart attack? And why is that shifty-looking character at the back door of the bank? Is he planning to make an unauthorized after-hours withdrawal?

That's a quick look at the scenery, structure, detailing phase of layout construction. I hope it's piqued your interest so that you'll want to learn more. There's a lot more to be said about scenery. The scope of the subject is so big that it would take a book to cover it adequately. In fact, several good books have been written on scenery building. One of the best is Dave Frary's *How to Build Realistic Model Railroad Scenery,* which is sold in many hobby shops.

FIG. 4-16. This is how the Muskego & Western looked with some structures temporarily in place and some scenery forms mocked up with crumpled-up newspapers.

EQUIPMENT SELECTION

For a small layout like this one I recommend that you choose short locomotives. (See **fig. 4-17.**) They'll look better and run better than their big brothers. That's because some brands of locomotives with long wheelbases bind on these sharp-radius (2-foot) curves. While all LGB locomotives, including the big ones, will operate on these tight curves, they look toylike due to the excessive equipment overhang.

Obviously, you can't run very long trains on a small layout like this. A freight train might consist of a locomotive, two cars, and a caboose. A passenger train could be simply a locomotive and a combine.

I hope I've convinced you that it is possible to build a nice large-scale layout in a relatively small space. Building and operating a layout like our Muskego & Western is a hobby activity the whole family can enjoy. Have fun!

FIG. 4-17. Short locomotives like these are the most suitable for use on a small layout such as the one described in this chapter.

CHAPTER FIVE

An Indoor Large Scale Empire

FIG. 5-1. Engine no. 453, a K-27-class 2-8-2, pulls the Durango passenger train into the Durango depot, while no. 50 does some switching chores in the yard. Both engines, the coaling tower, and the sand house were scratchbuilt by author Barry Bogs.

FIG. 5-2. Barry Bogs at the control panel of his Gn3 Colorado & Western layout. It's located in front of the Durango yard. Control is provided by the three Pacific Fast Mail throttle/steam sound systems shown, along with two walkaround throttles. The colorful main control panel was made from the side of an old copying machine. Photos in this chapter are by Bob Werre.

by Barry Bogs

My interest in model railroading can be traced to my early childhood. At the age of two I received a plastic pull train. By the time I was five I already had an HO scale train set. Over the years I built numerous HO layouts until I entered college. After graduation, I married Janet, a wonderfully understanding woman.

After we purchased a home, I wanted to get back into model railroading and thought I'd like to try a larger scale. I liked Denver & Rio Grande Western narrow gauge, and On3 looked like a great scale/gauge combination to me. However, with K-series locomotives approaching the $2,000 range, even my understanding wife said, "No way."

INTRODUCTION TO LGB

Then one day I happened upon an LGB catalog with those beautiful color pictures of D&RGW narrow gauge rolling stock. Here in Texas, "bigger is better" (usually), so these large scale (1:22.5 proportion) trains appealed to me. They're roughly twice as big as O scale and almost four times HO. Naturally, I assumed they were better.

I purchased a few LGB pieces and was very pleased with the quality. Somehow, these large scale pieces have a presence that those in smaller scales don't.

Operation, which at first was on the floor of our family room, was great because I spent more time railroading, rather than troubleshooting problems. Operation and switching was even better after Kadee introduced its large scale couplers.

When I started in 1986, there wasn't a large selection of American-style locomotives in Gn3, so I took a couple of LGB German-prototype locomotives and chopped them up to look like steam engines that could have run in America.

I installed the same PFM sound system that I'd used with my HO locomotives. I was pleasantly surprised at the sound quality out of the 3½" speakers. It was wonderful compared to the cut-down 1½" speakers in my HO engines. You need to experience this in person to understand just how realistic it is.

After months of my running trains on the family room floor, Janet said she was growing tired of stepping over the LGB track, so I started looking for another location.

I never considered putting it outside because I'm not a garden railroader and enjoy staying in air-conditioned comfort when the temperature outside is approaching 100 degrees here in Houston.

What I needed was a place to build a permanent layout indoors. Fortunately, our house has a very large attic, and that's where I focused my attention.

ROOM IN THE ATTIC

Starting on January 1, 1987, I worked evenings and weekends on the train room for approximately five months. By the time I was finished I had a nice room measuring about 17 x 39 feet. Now I was ready to begin work on my dream empire.

In 1986, I had picked up a copy of the book *Model Railroading with John Allen* (Kalmbach Publishing Co.). Between this book and the two-part article by Malcolm Furlow, "Adventures in G," published in the October and November 1986 issues of *Model Railroader,* I got all the inspiration I needed to build the Gn3 layout of my dreams.

I began with the basic premise that anything that could be done in HOn3 could be done in Gn3. This is still my approach. In fact, I continue to use HOn3 and some On3 items to build Gn3 models by scaling the dimensions up 3.87 from HOn3 and 2.14 from On3.

LAYOUT CONSTRUCTION BEGINS

I used traditional L-girder benchwork, which is so strong I can stand on it for easy access. The track is all handlaid on Homasote roadbed. I cut my own ties on a table saw and used Rail Craft's code 250 weathered rail, which I spiked in place with Life-Like HO spikes. I used Ramos rail joiners.

To ensure good electrical connections, I drilled holes through both rail and joiners for 2-56 brass screws. I soldered the power feeder wires to the brass screws.

I scratchbuilt my turnouts using epoxy frogs made in a homemade RTV mold. The turnouts are electrically operated by twin-coil switch machines mounted on Rix-Rax mounting brackets.

My handlaid track not only looks more realistic, but also costs about half as much as commercial track and turnouts.

The layout is wired for cab control. From the control panel, I can operate five trains simultaneously from PFM throttle/sound systems.

SCENERY AND STRUCTURES

I relied on the hardshell method of scenery construction. To the basic hardshell I applied plaster rock castings and colored them using acrylic paints. I used Colorado red dirt and ground foam for the texture.

Tree moss worked great for bushes, and hemp rope did fine for weeds. I built more than 800 trees using a variety of techniques. The tallest trees were made by shaving dowel rods to a point, wire-brushing them to simulate bark texture, and staining them. Then I dipped the ends of plomosa fern in white glue and inserted them into small holes drilled into the trunk. I made the shorter, dense trees out of furnace filters and ground foam. I used pepper grass for the aspens.

All the bridges, except for the LGB spans, were scratchbuilt from 1" x 12" white wood that I sawed on a table saw. I used 1⁄16" brass rods, with 2mm nuts and washers slipped over the ends for the truss rods. At first glance, people think the rods are threaded. I used Atlas track nails to simulate bridge rivets.

FIG. 5-3. Number 453 has just taken on coal here at Durango. As soon as the servicing has been completed, the engine will be turned and ready for another passenger run. On the high line in the background we see the Silverton heading downgrade from its namesake city of Silverton, Colorado.

FIG. 5-4. The turntable is in place and operating, and a scratchbuilt roundhouse will be added soon. Locomotive no. 234, easing into the turntable, is a scratchbuilt model of a D&RGW class C-16 engine.

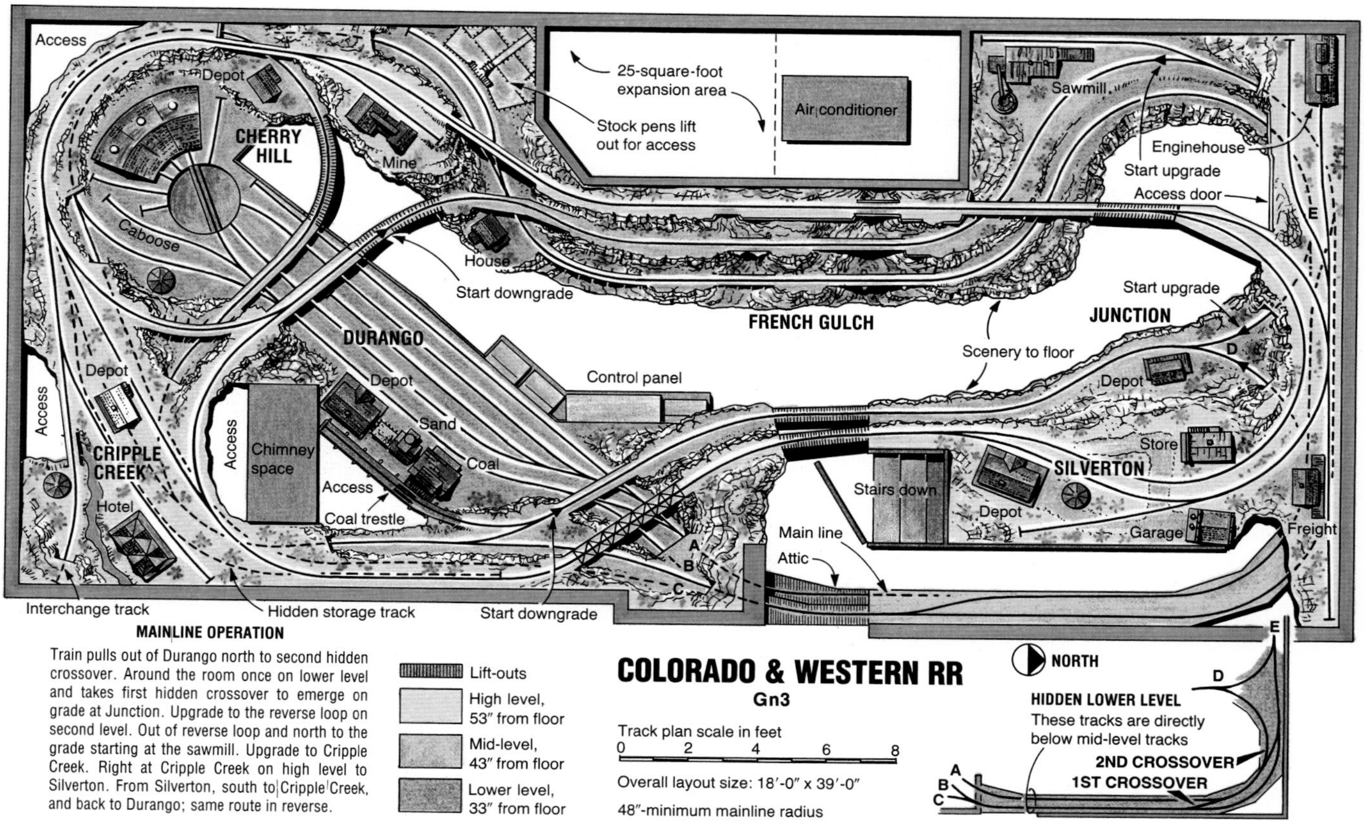

Access
Depot
CHERRY HILL
Mine
25-square-foot expansion area
Stock pens lift out for access
Air conditioner
Sawmill
Enginehouse
Start upgrade
Access door
E
Caboose
House
Start downgrade
FRENCH GULCH
Start upgrade
JUNCTION
Scenery to floor
D
DURANGO
Depot
Control panel
Depot
Access
Access
Chimney space
Sand
Coal
Access
Coal trestle
Depot
CRIPPLE CREEK
Hotel
Store
SILVERTON
Stairs down
Depot
Garage
Freight
Main line
Attic
A
B
C
Interchange track
Hidden storage track
Start downgrade
MAINLINE OPERATION
Train pulls out of Durango north to second hidden crossover. Around the room once on lower level and takes first hidden crossover to emerge on grade at Junction. Upgrade to the reverse loop on second level. Out of reverse loop and north to the grade starting at the sawmill. Upgrade to Cripple Creek. Right at Cripple Creek on high level to Silverton. From Silverton, south to Cripple Creek, and back to Durango; same route in reverse.
Lift-outs
High level, 53″ from floor
Mid-level, 43″ from floor
Lower level, 33″ from floor
COLORADO & WESTERN RR
Gn3
Track plan scale in feet
0 2 4 6 8
Overall layout size: 18′-0″ x 39′-0″
48″-minimum mainline radius
NORTH
HIDDEN LOWER LEVEL
These tracks are directly below mid-level tracks
2ND CROSSOVER
1ST CROSSOVER
E
D
A
B
C

FIG. 5-5. Track plan of the Colorado & Western.

The majority of the buildings are commercial items by Pola. However, I did scratchbuild the coal and sand towers, the roundhouse, and the coal mine structures.

SCRATCHBUILDING LOCOMOTIVES

Most of the rolling stock on the layout is LGB equipment. I attribute the reliability of operation on my layout to the fine quality of these narrow gauge locomotives and cars. Even so, some of the models I wanted weren't available from any manufacturer. As a result, I had to do some scratchbuilding.

I've found scratchbuilding Gn3 locomotives to be the most rewarding aspect of the hobby. The models are easy to handle, and you don't need tweezers to put one together. And at the end of an evening, my eyes aren't tired from squinting.

Rio Grande
453
COLORADO AND WESTERN

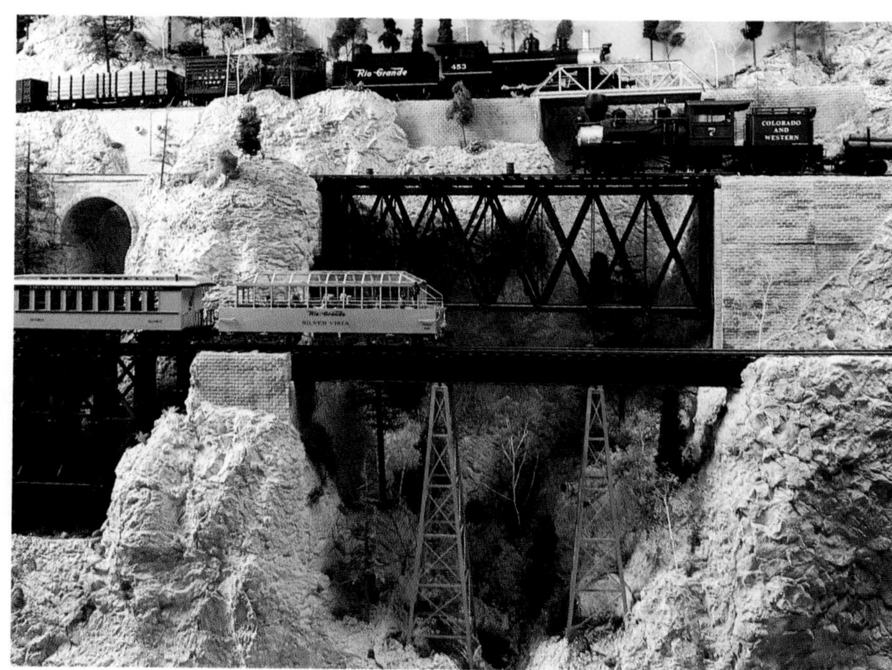

FIG. 5-6 The first thing visitors see is this scene inspired by French Gulch on John Allen's legendary HO scale Gorre & Daphetid. The Silver Vista observation car was scratchbuilt by the author.

FIG. 5-7. On the upper track a crowd has gathered at the Silverton station, waiting for the arriving passenger train to Durango. The author based his scratchbuilt Shay, shown pulling a long train below, on Model Die Casting's HOn3 model.

Styrene is my material of choice because of the availability of shapes and ease of use.

The D&RGW class K-27 2-8-2 and the no. 50 diesel bodies were scratchbuilt and powered by LGB drives. Years after I scratchbuilt my model of D&RGW no. 50, LGB introduced one to its line. The Shay is based on Model Die Casting's HOn3 Shay. It's powered by two LGB tender drives used for European-prototype locomotives. I used ring and pinion gears and ball-bearing races from a radio-controlled car to hold the drive shafts in place.

COUPLERS

I use Kadee couplers, which I've found to be very reliable. I truck-mount them close to the body of the car to get the most realistic look possible. After trying both truck-mounting and body-mounting, I can say that the former works better for me because of the sharp curves. I use 48" minimum radius, which is approximately the same as LGB's 1600-series curved track.

Kadee permanent magnets have been installed for uncoupling in all sidings and in the yard. Out on the main lines I use their no. 810 O scale electric uncoupling ramps. The metal wings have to be spread apart slightly, but they seem to be fairly reliable.

THE FUTURE

Most visitors think my railroad is complete. But every model railroader knows a layout is never finished, and mine is no exception. There are so many projects I want to complete.

There's a waybill system that I plan to implement to enhance the operation. I also plan to build a roundhouse and two coal mines and to add more detail throughout the entire layout. When that's complete I plan to expand the train room further into the attic!

FIG 5-8. Our photographer caught action on three levels in this shot. At the top we see no. 234 crossing the highest bridge on the railroad. On the middle level a log train is headed for the mill, and coming toward us on the lowest level is a slow freight. In this area of the layout the scenery extends from the floor to the ceiling, thereby creating the feel of Colorado narrow gauge country.

CHAPTER SIX

Introduction to Garden Railroading

by Marc Horovitz

Garden railroading is the art of combining a model railroad and a beautiful garden to create a railroad-like atmosphere. The difference between a traditional indoor layout and a garden railway is the difference between realism and reality. Indoors, the goal is to create the illusion of reality through the use of artificial materials—mountains are made of plaster, rivers are made of plastic resin, etc. Outdoors, you are dealing with real life—reality. Hills are made of dirt, rivers are made of water, rocks are made of stone. (See **fig. 6-2.**) This can be both a blessing and a curse. Washouts can cause problems, snow can stop trains, and trees and branches can fall on the track. But when you compare these minor nuisances to the joys of having a real (albeit small) railroad at your doorstep that is constantly growing

Fig. 6-1 (above). Dean and Sharon Lowe's California garden railway is a wonderful collaboration between a gardener and a railroader. All rolling stock is weathered. The tunnel portal and bridge are scratchbuilt. The dry creek beneath the bridge is lined with cement.

Fig. 6-2 (right). A 44-ton diesel takes a short freight train through the canyon on Dick Schafer's Galena Railway & Navigation Company line. The rock is native Colorado granite and sandstone.

and changing with the seasons, the weather, and even the time of day, this seems a small price to pay. Most people even consider it to be part of the fun.

GETTING STARTED

Before you begin to plan your garden railroad, there are several things to consider. Examine the area your line will occupy to see if it's suitable. Here are some of the questions you should ask yourself:

• **Is your area secure?** Vandalism can be a problem in some areas. What is out of sight is out of mind, and a high, opaque fence may be a good idea. (See **fig. 6-3.**) On the other hand, if the neighborhood you live in is itself secure, fences may not be necessary. Several garden railways have been built in front yards, in full sight of the neighbors and all passersby, with never a problem.

When you're not running your railroad, bring your trains—and sometimes buildings and other structures—indoors. You could even secure them in permanent garden structures of their own, like solid engine houses or train sheds. These will prevent them from being damaged by weather or from wandering off when you aren't home. Although security is not something to be paranoid about, it should be considered.

• **Is your area more or less level?** Levelness is not mandatory in building an outdoor railroad, but the topography of your land can seriously affect the configuration of the railroad that is built on it. The steepness of the grade a train can negotiate is limited, and if your yard is quite hilly, it may need to be smoothed out some.

You can do this leveling with additional earth made into embankments, retaining walls to prevent soil from washing away, or bridgework and trestlework to span larger or deeper gaps.

• **Is there an existing garden, or will the garden be designed along with the railway?** Consider the garden as part of the railroad. If a garden exists already, consider how to integrate the railroad into it so as to show each to its best advantage, while creating the kind of environment and atmosphere for your trains that you desire.

FIG. 6-3. Two trains meet on the trestles on Herb Chaudiere's Cranis Garden Railway in Washington State. All bridgework is scratchbuilt. The upper locomotive is a modified Kalamazoo engine, and the lower one is a detailed and weathered LGB product. Note the fence in the background, which secures the area.

If you will design a new garden, plan it along with the railway. You should have a clear picture in your mind as to what you want your line to be. If you are weak in gardening, do some homework—it will pay off later. Visit local nurseries, read books, and talk to people.

• **Are there things in the way—like clotheslines, houses, or swimming pools—that must be removed or worked around?** If so, these things can influence the route of the track. You can cross a sidewalk at ground level by cutting away the concrete, laying in the track, and replacing the concrete with new cement, being careful to allow for flangeways. It's possible to cross a walkway above ground level with a lift-out or movable bridge. However, when you are operating, liftout sections will be obstructions.

You can build around swimming pools, but they tend to be a visual distraction to the railroad. If the line is close to the pool, it may be difficult to photograph without getting the pool in the shot, too.

Build around (or through) other structures, as well. Many garden railways begin indoors and then go out through a hole in the wall. Some are routed through garden sheds, where the trains are stored and serviced.

• **How elaborate will the line be?** As a general rule in building a garden railroad, less is more. A traditional indoor layout may have many loops of track, dozens of engines, and hundreds of pieces of rolling stock.

Outdoors, where we are dealing with the elements, a single-track mainline usually suffices, with sidings at stations, industries, and points of interest, and perhaps a branch line to an outlying terminal. A garden line will have a much different look than an indoor line. To get started, a single locomotive and three or four pieces of rolling stock—freight or passenger—are all you really need.

CHOOSING EQUIPMENT

Before choosing a first train, decide what your railroad is to be. Is it a line that will haul only freight? A line of this nature might start out with one or two small engines and maybe a half dozen freight cars of specific purpose. Or perhaps you

FIG. 6-4. All three of these structures on the Siedelmans' garden line in Colorado were scratchbuilt and weathered by owners Lynn and Jim. The depot is a scale model of its prototype in Jefferson, Colorado. Trains and track are from LGB. Plantings, like the 'Dragon's Blood' sedum in foreground, are especially suited to their hot, dry setting.

prefer a passenger line that connects small towns? Again, a single engine (and maybe another for backup) and three or four coaches would be enough to get a railroad like this off the ground. (See **fig. 6-4.**)

Is your line an old-fashioned narrow gauge steam railroad, or a modern, standard gauge, diesel-powered line? The space you have available may help to answer these questions. A small industrial line, with little engines, short cars, and tight curves, will fit better and look more at home in a limited space. A modern mainline road with A-B-A diesel lash-ups and trains of twenty or more cars will require broader curves and longer straight stretches to look right. Do your homework. Read books and magazines on the subject before jumping in.

Your budget is a consideration when starting out, though if it is your aspiration to ultimately own a sprawling railroad empire, don't compromise that dream by initially purchasing equipment that doesn't fit in with your plans just because it is cheap. It is ultimately more gratifying to realize your hopes, even if you must do so in small steps.

Consider the nationality of the railroad. If this is not important to you, your choice of equipment is considerably broadened. However, if you prefer to run American prototypes, examine the market carefully to see if what you need is commercially available. You may have to make or modify equipment to suit your needs.

TRACK

There is a wide range of commercially available track today, and this is probably the best approach for the novice. When you have gained some experience, you might want to consider building your own track.

Commercial track is available in short pieces of set lengths and curvatures—called sectional track—or in longer sections that you can bend to suit your own needs. Sectional track is good for some applications, but it can be very limiting.

Sectional track is an excellent choice if your railway is not to be permanent, as it can be easily picked up and put down at will. Sectional curved track of several different radii is available. LGB's 1100 is the tightest curve, at 2' radius. Their middle-radius track (1500) has a 2' 6" radius, and the company's widest-radius track (1600) has a radius of 3' 10". When used together, these curved tracks of different radii make it easy to create parallel main lines.

Straight track comes in different lengths, nominally 1-foot, 2-foot, and 3-foot sections. They can be easily cut to fit with a hacksaw if they are the wrong size. LGB even makes an expandable section to take up a little slack.

Turnouts are offered with diverging tracks of two different radii, to match LGB's 1100 and 1600 curves.

For a permanent railway you should consider using flexible track. You can bend it to any desired curvature and make your railway go where it should go, not where it may have to go with sectional track.

Several companies on the market today offer flexible track. Micro Engineering offers track in both code 250 and 332 aluminum rail and nickel silver, a brass alloy. (The code number of rail is nothing more than the height of the rail measured in thousandths of an inch. Thus, code 250 rail is .250"—or 1/4"—tall.) Garich Light Transport has flexible gauge 1 track with code 250 brass rail, in both 1:24 (visually compatible with 1:22.5) and 1:32 scales. The difference between the two different products is the size, shape, and spacing of the ties. Llagas Creek Railways has 1:32 scale gauge 1 track with code 250 aluminum, nickel silver, or steel rail, and of course LGB has its own flexible track with plastic tie strips to match their sectional track, using code 332 brass rail. Several other companies, including Aristo-Craft, Bachmann, Lionel, Gargraves, Märklin, Peco, Brandbright, Old Pullman, Tenmille, and others also offer gauge 1 track.

The term "flex track" is a little misleading. In the smaller scales—HO, for instance—flex track can be easily bent to shape and applied to the roadbed. In the larger sizes of rail, particularly code 332 brass, the rail is heavy enough to be considered a structural section. You can't just lay a piece of track on the ground and bend it to shape. It will spend the rest of its life trying to unbend and will eventually succeed.

Prebend the rail used in flex track to the proper configuration before sliding it into the plastic tie strips. With aluminum rail, you can often do this by careful hand-bending (wear leather gloves). For the best curves, however, use a machine designed for the purpose, like a commercially available railbender. It is surprising how attainable smooth and accurate curves can be with a machine like this.

HANDLAID TRACK

The ultimate trackwork, though, is the track that you build yourself, using real wood ties and metal spikes to hold the rails in place. You not only choose where the track is to go, but you also determine how it looks.

Tie size, shape, and spacing will greatly affect the appearance of your track. (See **fig. 6-5.**) Also, in the garden, you may want to make your ties fairly thick, to give more surface area for the ballast to grip. Ties two to three times as deep as they are wide are not uncommon. Switches, dual-gauge track, and other special types of trackwork can be easily accommodated with handlaid track, giving your railroad a homogeneous look, like a full-size line.

If you handlay track in smaller scales, you know that it is usually done in place, with the ties glued down to the baseboard and the rail spiked on after the glue has set. When building larger scale track for outdoor use, it is tedious, difficult, and pointless to try to build the track in place. It is much simpler to build track on a workbench, using a homemade jig to hold the ties in place while the rails are spiked to them. You'll probably want to build several curved jigs, one for each radius, and maybe even one or two with transition curves in them. Use curved jigs in conjunction with one another and also in conjunction with straight jigs when assembling long sections of rail that include both straight and curved sections of track. Since the trackwork *is* the railroad, you can never spend too much time getting it right.

Ties should be made of a rot-resistant wood. Redwood and cedar are two commonly used and widely available materials. Pressure-treated pine can also be used, but be sure that the pressure treatment extends all the way into the wood you are using. For instance, if you are cutting up 4 x 4s, the chemicals may only extend an inch or so into the wood. Pressure-treated wood can produce toxic dust when sawn, so take proper precautions.

If your ties are made of a particularly tough wood, you may want to predrill the holes for each spike, about half the depth of the spike. This will ease insertion, resulting in fewer bent spikes and frayed nerves.

When spiking, hold the rails in place with a track gauge. A three-point gauge is best because, when used properly, it provides for a slight amount of gauge widening on curves. Roll gauges can also be

FIG. 6-5. This is Dean and Sharon Lowe's line in Southern California. Close attention has been paid to trackwork and to structure and plant placement to create realistic and plausible scenes. The trains are mostly kitbashed and modified LGB.

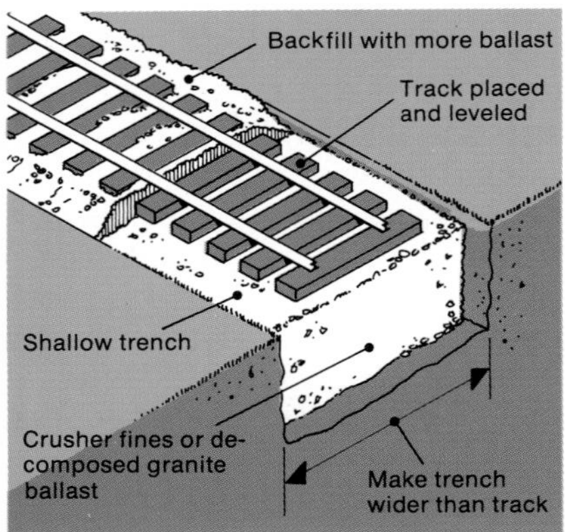

FLOAT THE TRACK IN BALLAST

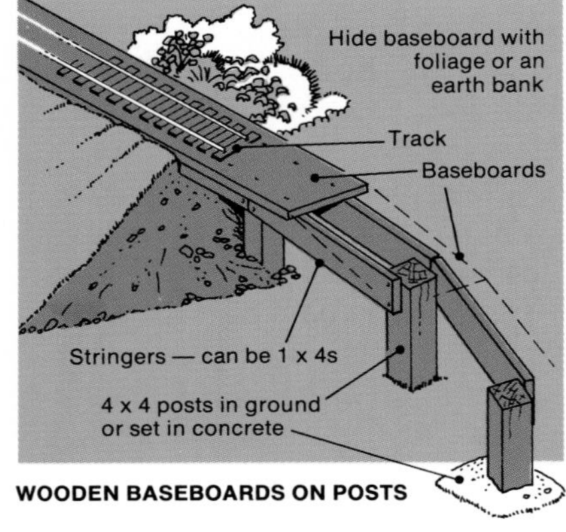

WOODEN BASEBOARDS ON POSTS

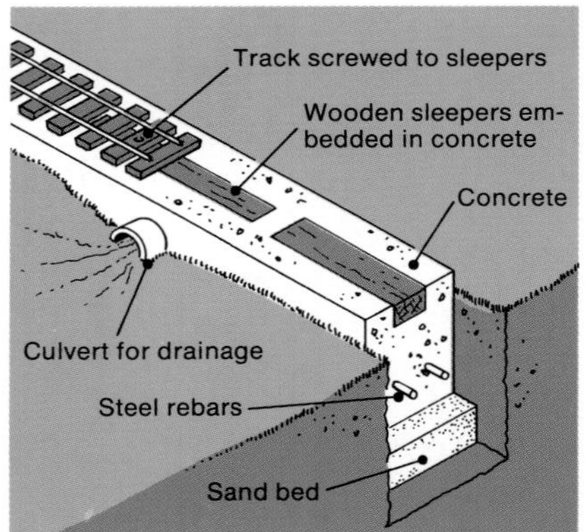

CONCRETE ROADBED

used. You'll want another gauge, which can be nothing more than a scrap of metal or cardboard that is as wide as the distance between the outside edge of the rail and the edge of the tie. This dimension is contingent on the width of your ties and the gauge of your track.

When building the track, spike one rail in its entirety first, and then come back and spike the second (and third, if you are building dual-gauge track). Use your little gauge to position the rail the proper distance in from the end of the tie, and spike it at one end. Then do the same at the other end, and then in the middle. Keep subdividing the spaces, and you'll end up with a nice smooth curve, or a dead straight section, properly spaced in from the end of the tie. Once the first rail is securely in position, the second rail is a snap.

When a piece of track is lifted from the jig, it will be a little unstable. The individual ties may tend to slide or shift, or your curve may tend to relax a little. One way to solve this problem is to nail battens—longitudinal strips—to the underside of the ties. These strips, which can be made from scrap wood, will hold the ties in position, which will then hold the rail in its proper configuration. When it's in place in the ballast, the battens will be concealed, and your track will be very strong and stable. Building your own track is a lot of work, and your railroad may not progress as fast as you'd like it to, but handlaid track is well worth the time spent.

PLANNING THE LINE

What is the best minimum radius to use on your railroad? There is no "best," really. The rule of thumb is to use the widest minimum that will conveniently and aesthetically fit in your available space. I like a minimum of at least 6 feet (making a 12-foot circle), but fine railroads have been built with sharper curves. On the other hand, long standard gauge passenger trains running at speed just don't look right twisting around very tight curves, even though they may be capable of doing so. A minimum radius of 10 feet may be called for in this case, and a really grand curve could be as wide as 15 feet or 20 feet.

However, track of very tight radius was sometimes used on prototypical railroads, especially in the narrow gauges. Industrial railroads that ran very small equipment and had to thread their lines between buildings or along ledges used extremely tight curves. Several manufacturers of industrial railway equipment even offered full-size sectional track so that temporary railroads (those used in the construction of a dam, for instance) could be easily put down, moved at will, and taken up when the job was complete. Remember that your railroad will be more plausible if you tailor your rolling stock to your curves.

Try not to make grades steeper than about 3 percent. Steep grades are unrealistic and will severely limit your train length. In prototype practice it is considered that train length is cut in half for every percentage of grade that must be negotiated. So if a locomotive can pull an eight-car train on level track, it will only be able to manage four cars on a 1 percent grade, two cars on a 2 percent grade, and one car on a 3 percent grade. On a 4 percent

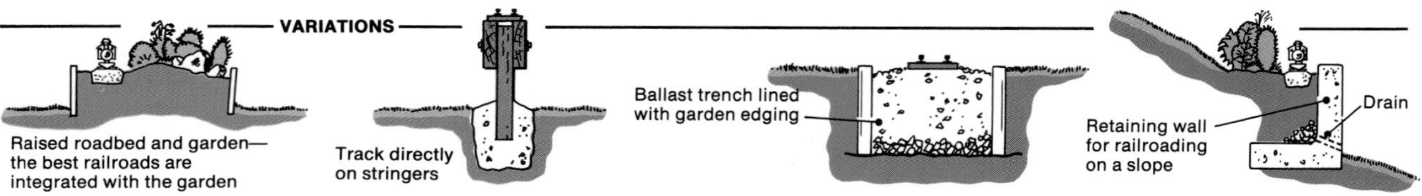

FIG. 6-6. Roadbed construction methods for garden railroads.

grade, another locomotive must be added to get that single car up.

On model railroads, however, electrically powered engines will pull unrealistically long trains up unrealistically steep inclines. But for plausible operation, apply the above rule of thumb.

Other factors will affect your engine's ability to tote a train up a hill. It will be far easier if the entire grade is on straight track. Wheel flanges binding the rails will slow a train on curves, particularly tight curves. The condition of the bearings on your rolling stock is another factor. Also, wheels of different materials and profiles have different rolling characteristics. Companies such as Gary Raymond offer well-designed metal wheels as replacements for all the currently available plastic wheelsets. While metal wheels do add weight to the car, the improved rolling characteristics more than compensate for it.

*FIG. 6-7. **If you want a solid foundation for your track, build it like those used for full-size structures. The track for Steve and Judy Arrigotti's Mother Lode Garden Railway shown here is set on a concrete foundation. Photo by Steven Arrigotti.***

ROADBED

There are probably as many different methods of building roadbed in the garden as there are garden railroaders. There is no right or wrong way to do it, though some ways may be better than others, depending on where you live.

Perhaps the best general-purpose advice for most applications is to build your railway in a prototypical manner. On a full-size railroad, the track actually floats in the ballast. By floating the track in the ballast, you allow it to move. Summer heat will cause the rails to expand, and winter cold will make them contract. The spring thaw may bring frost heave. Floating track will move as it needs to, but will be easy to realign when necessary (probably once or twice a year, if that).

Dig a shallow trench—say 2" to 3" deep, and a little wider than your track—and fill it with ballast up to just below grade level, as shown in **fig. 6-6.** There is no need to line the trench with plastic or anti-weed fabric. On the contrary, good drainage is very important and an underlayment may impede it. Place your track on the ballast and level it up, making sure it's exactly where you want it. Backfill with more ballast to the tops of the ties, which should be at grade. Tamp the ballast into place for a better fit, using a spare tie or a piece of wood to push the ballast down between each tie. Fill in again where necessary.

A word about ballast: Pea gravel is often used for ballast, but it is not the best choice. Pea gravel is a type of river rock, and the stones are round, so they tend to roll. A heavy rain will wash the gravel away, as will the lawn sprinkler.

What you need is a stone with sharp points and edges. These teeth will lock the ballast (and track) into place. Many people use a product called "crusher fines," available from local rockyards. It is chipped granite, and it contains a fair amount of rock dust, which is an added advantage. After the track has been firmly set in the ballast, the roadbed can be sprinkled with water. The rock dust sets up like cement, but it is still easy to break apart for relocating or releveling the track. A good alternative to crusher fines is chicken grit, available in several different sizes at grain and feed stores.

Fig. 6-6 also shows other methods of roadbed construction. One is to elevate the track on a wooden baseboard, which can be attached to wooden posts sunk in the ground—but only in temperate climates. Frost heave in the colder climes will force the stakes out of the ground during the spring thaw, making your railroad look like a roller coaster. If you live in a cold place and want to try this idea, set the posts securely in concrete, or make sure they penetrate to below the frost line. Use a rot-resistant wood like redwood or cedar, or pressure-treated wood intended for use in decks and patios.

If you are planning never to move (or change your track plan) the railway can be set on a concrete foundation. (See **fig. 6-7.**) Make the roadbed in much the same way as the foundation of a house, with steel reinforcing rods to prevent it from cracking. It is essential that your form work be of the highest quality. Smooth curves and consistent grades are important. Screw the track to wooden tie-downs embedded in the surface of the concrete. The surface of the concrete roadbed can be at grade and disguised with ballast, or it can be elevated slightly. If it is elevated, it will act as a dam, so be sure that you have cast-in culverts at the low points to allow for proper drainage.

experience from running an electrically powered train. If you approach it expecting the same sort of performance and instantaneous availability that you get with an electric engine, you may be disappointed. Every steam locomotive is different—even two locomotives of the same type made by the same manufacturer. Operators must learn the performance idiosyncrasies of a large scale steam loco, just as with a full-size steam loco, to know what it is capable of, and what sort of train it will take over what sort of terrain. We'll leave live steam for now, but it will be discussed more in depth in Chapter 9.

Clockwork. Another more esoteric alternative in the garden is clockwork. It was once the most prevalent form of power, though it is little seen today. Very fine scale locomotives were built, primarily in Britain and other European countries, that derived their power from a large spring. Clockwork was never a serious alternative for the serious modeler in this country, as nearly all spring-driven trains made over here were low-end toys.

However, a clockwork engine or two can be great fun. You can get old Marx mechanisms that, when resized to gauge 1, can provide a mechanism for a little industrial switcher or the like. I've even heard of mechanisms being ganged together to power 2-4-4-2s!

LANDSCAPING AND SCENERY

As stated elsewhere, it is the goal of the garden railroader to achieve a railroad-like atmosphere through the integration of railroad and garden. (See **fig. 6-9.**) "Garden" does not mean just plantings—though they are of paramount importance—but all the additional landscaping that must be done to attain the desired goal. Much of what should be done is determined by your existing topography, how accessible you want your railroad to be (that is, will it lie at grade, or will the ground level and the garden be elevated for convenience or to smooth out the hills?), and how much you intend to modify the area in which you are working.

Placing Rock and Dirt. Moving landscaping materials is hard work, but it usually has to be done only once. If your line expands later, you will have done the major work at the beginning. If you intend to include a rock garden, or even a few stone outcroppings to suggest a mountainous region, plan these areas right from the beginning. Don't add them as an afterthought.

Rocks can be had from rockyards, or they can be trapped in the wild. If you set out cross-country on a rock-gathering expedition, be sure that the area you are invading is not someone else's property, a state or national park, or some other area where removal of things of local geological interest is prohibited. The rockyard sells stone by the pound. Its price will vary depending on how attractive or scarce the stone is. Chose your rocks carefully; generally, a natural outcropping will consist of only one type of stone. Select rocks of different sizes, too. Stones all of the same size will be boring to work with if you are trying to create an interesting setting. A variety of sizes will add interest and challenge your design skills. (See **fig. 6-10.**) Read books on rock gardening that discuss rock placement. It isn't as easy as you might think.

Of course, there are exceptions to every rule, and the one that comes to mind in rock placement is Norm Grant's now-defunct South Park & San Juan in Colorado. Norm used many different kinds of stone on his railroad, but he got away with it because of the way the stone was used and because his line was big. In one area he used carefully selected white sandstones, artfully combined to form a cliff face. In other areas, he used granite, worn with age and covered with moss, to create natural-looking outcroppings. And in another large area, jagged granite rip-rap created a small scale illusion of the Rocky Mountains. The areas were separated by expanses of level track, planting, tunnels, or other visual barriers. It worked. But you must understand the rules before you can successfully break them.

You can often get dirt for nothing. Watch for "Free fill dirt" signs on telephone poles near construction areas. The advantage to this dirt, of course, is that it's free. There are several disadvantages, however. A big one is that you must haul it yourself. Another is

*FIG. 6-9. A train of USA Trains rolling stock is headed up by a 44-tonner, built by Alan Olson, on Marc and Barb Horovitz's Ogden Botanical Railway. The track is handlaid using LGB code 332 brass rail spiked to redwood ties. Pine-leaf penstemon (*Penstemon pinifolius*) borders the track at right. At left,* Nierembergia *'Purple Robe' and white sweet alyssum yield summer color. Photo by Barbara Horovitz.*

FIG. 6-10. A mixed train rolls through the cut on Jim and Kevin Strong's Woodland Railway in Maryland. This line features exceptionally careful, creative use of plant material, and battery-powered and live-steam operation. Photo by Kevin Strong.

that you don't really know what you are getting. Are there chunks of concrete or broken glass hidden inside? Is it full of weed seeds that will sprout later on when you are trying to establish your garden? What's it made of? Is it mostly sand or mostly clay, or a little of each?

The alternative is to buy dirt from a garden center. Dirt is sold by the yard. A yard of dirt is actually a cubic yard, or 27 cubic feet. If you are filling a space between two retaining walls, it may be fairly easy to calculate how much dirt you need. On the other hand, if you are building hills and valleys, it might be quite difficult. The cost of dirt will vary. High-grade potting soil or topsoil will probably be the most expensive, and dirt that is mostly sand or clay will be the cheapest.

It is usually well worth the nominal charge to have the dirt delivered to your house by a dump truck.

Once your yard is filled with mountains of dirt and piles of rocks, then what? That's when the hard work begins. You must now start shifting the dirt and placing the rocks so that your grand plan is realized. Rock placement is perhaps the most difficult task, both physically and aesthetically. I've known people to reposition a rock weighing over a ton three, four, or more times, usually with the assistance of a crane, to make sure it is just right. After all, it may rest where you put it for centuries. Do it right the first time. To paraphrase an old adage, plant rocks in haste, repent at leisure.

The dirt can be built up until it looks right or fulfills its function. Compared to rocks, dirt is easy to move around, so don't hesitate to change your mind. You can change it later, too, if you must. It has been suggested by experienced garden railroaders that you should get the dirt where you want it and then come back in a year and build the railway. During this year the dirt will have settled and compacted about as much as it's going to, and you will have a steady and stable surface for your roadbed.

Of course, if you don't want to wait a year—and who among us does—there are things you can do to speed the process. Tamping the dirt is a must, and your hardware store will have a special tool for this. It is nothing more than a heavy chunk of metal at the end of a pole. I suggest thoroughly tamping the route of the track and then giving it a good watering. Do this about three times in as many days, and you should have a relatively stable track bed. There will always be some shifting, but it can usually be compensated for with the roadbed.

MULCH AND THE GARDEN

Leaving great areas of exposed dirt lying around is just asking for trouble. If you are building an extensive line, I suggest that you do it in small steps, finishing off one area before going on to the next. If you build an entire set of foothills in your yard and then neglect them, the first thing you know they'll be covered with weeds. And they'll also be subject to erosion the first time it rains, leaving you with unplanned gullies and mud flats. The dirt must be covered.

Grass in the form of sod is a reasonable expedient, even if you don't ultimately plan to have grass there. Another good plan is to use mulch. (See **fig. 6-11.**) It can be bark chips, small stones, wood chippings, or other things. The mulch will prevent light from reaching the ground, thus inhibiting the growth of weeds. Water will gently seep through the mulch and not erode the exposed earth.

FIG. 6-11. A steam train pauses to take on water. Note how Russ Larson uses mulch along the right-of-way to ensure that the line doesn't erode when it gets "watered."

FIG. 6-12. A lot of railroad is packed into a small space on Fran and Carl Pfetzing's California line. A footbridge carries pedestrians over the track to a gazebo. Every square inch of this line has been carefully thought out. Photo by Marc Horovitz.

Of course, you'll ultimately want to cover the dirt with suitable plants—the garden. Many beautiful and effective garden railways have been created by people who claim not to be gardeners. Gardening is a fascinating aspect to the hobby, and railway gardening has become a sub-hobby in its own right. It is often the garden that ties the separate elements of the railroad together and draws entire families into garden railroading.

It is impossible in a book of this nature to educate you about the myriad aspects of gardening, or even to give you a comprehensive list of plants that grow well in your area. We have included a generalized list of plants that will give you a starting point. A good source of information is your local rock garden society. Rock-garden plants go especially well with garden railways. Go to garden centers, read gardening magazines and books, and visit public and private gardens in your area.

When choosing plants for the railway, consider the function the plant must serve. (See **fig. 6-12.**) Do you want something that imitates a lawn for the yards around the houses? How about a plant that can be planted in multiples in a line as an informal miniature hedge? Small trees can be used en masse to suggest a forest, or a single fine specimen can be used to emphasize an important point on the line.

Plants in great diversity can be used to soften the rock garden and fill in the areas between the stones. If you have an area that needs filling in quickly, you might consider a more "invasive" plant. Slow-growing plants can be added later, and the invasive ones then removed.

Pay attention to the scale of the plants. As they grow, you don't want to spend all of your free time trimming those that become too large for their settings.

As a general rule, there are three zones of planting in the garden railway. Plants near the track should be closely in scale with the trains, people, and buildings. As you get farther from the model setting, or in places where the trains pass through more rural areas, the plants can be larger—though you might want to continue using plants with smaller-scale components (leaves, branch structure, etc.). Back from this area, the plants can be as big as you like, as these very large plants will provide a pleasant green backdrop for the garden railroad.

Now that you have a grass-roots introduction to garden railroading, go outside and enjoy this exceedingly gratifying aspect of the hobby.

A Selection of Small Scale Plants for the Railway Garden

Use this list of suggestions as a guide in selecting miniature landscape material suited to your geographic location, climate, and railway theme. These selections are not necessarily considered the finest species or cultivars available; they are merely representative of the astounding array of possibilities. There are countless other dwarf, low-, and slow-growing plants available through local specialty nurseries and mail-order sources.

Fellow railway gardeners, your mail-order catalog descriptions, local cooperative extension service, botanical garden staff, or plant societies can help you determine the appropriateness of plants for your area. List compiled by Barbara Horovitz.

Mosslike carpeters for miniature lawns and meadows

Sagina subulata; S.s. 'Aurea'
Irish moss; Scotch moss

Scleranthus biflorus
New Zealand polster

Scleranthus uniflorus
New Zealand polster (bronzy)

True moss is also used, transplanted as "sod" from moist, shady settings.

Shrubby or low-growing mats, creepers, and weepers (nonconiferous)

Achillea tomentosa
Woolly yarrow

Adiantum venustum
Maidenhair fern

Alyssum montanum
Mountain basket-of-gold

Andromeda polifolia 'Nana'
Miniature bog andromeda, bog rosemary

Antennaria parvifolia 'McClintock'
Miniature pussytoes

Arenaria balearica
Corsican sandwort

Athyrium nipponicum 'Pictum'
Japanese painted fern

Aubrieta deltoidea
Rock cress; many named varieties

Calluna vulgaris
Scotch heather; all named varieties suitable

Cerastium tomentosum
Snow-in-summer

Cotoneaster apiculatus 'Tom Thumb'
Tom Thumb cotoneaster, min. cranberry cotoneaster

Cotula potentillina
Brass buttons

Delosperma nubigenum (D. congestum)
Yellow hardy iceplant

Dianthus gratianopolitanus 'Tiny Rubies'
Miniature cheddar pinks

Erica carnea
Spring heath; all named varieties suitable

Euonymus fortunei 'Kewensis' (E. f. 'Minima')
Kew euonymus, miniature winter-creeper

Ficus pumila
Creeping fig

Genista pilosa
Hairy greenweed, dwarf broom; many named varieties

Herniaria glaba
Rupturewort

Isotoma fluviatilis (*Laurentia fluviatilis*)
Blue-star creeper

Mentha requienii
Corsican mint

Muehlenbeckia axillaris
Creeping wire vine

Ophiopogon japonicus 'Kioto'
Miniature lilyturf; dwarf mondo grass

Paxistima canbyi (sometimes spelled Pachystima)
Canby paxistima, mountain lover

Phlox subulata
Creeping phlox; many varieties

Raoulia australis
New Zealand scab plant (silver)

Raoulia lutescens
New Zealand scab plant (golden)

Rosmarinus officinalis
Rosemary; all types fine, some are upright

Sedum acre 'Aureum'
Gold-moss sedum, golden carpet

Sedum album micranthum
White stonecrop variety

Sedum dasyphyllum

Sedum hispanicum (*S. glaucum*)
Spanish sedum

Sedum reflexum
Blue-spruce sedum or stonecrop

Sedum spathulifolium 'Cape Blanco' (sometimes 'Capa Blanca')
Cape Blanco sedum

Sempervivum arachnoideum
Cobweb houseleek or hen-and-chicks

Silene acaulis
Moss campion

Soleirolia soleirolii
Baby's tears

Tanacetum densum amani (*Chrysanthemum densum amani*)
Partridge feather

Thymus x citriodorus
Lemon thyme

Thymus pseudolanuginosus
Woolly thyme

Thymus serpyllum 'Minus'
Minus thyme, miniature thyme

Thymus spp.
Every species and variety of thyme excellent

Veronica liwanensis
Turkish veronica

Veronica pectinata 'Rosea'
Pink woolly veronica

Other miscellaneous finescale perennials

Armeria maritima
Thrift, sea pink

Artemisia frigida
Dwarf sage

Artemisia schmidtiana 'Silver Mound'
Silver mound sage

Artemisia x 'Powis Castle'
Powis Castle (Welsh) artemisia

Festuca ovina glauca
Blue sheep's-fescue

Sisyrinchium montanum
Blue-eyed grass

Little trees and upright shrubs, nonconiferous

Acer palmatum dissectum 'Red Filigree Lace'
Dwarf red laceleaf Japanese maple

Betula alba 'Trost's Dwarf'
Dwarf white birch

Betula nana
Dwarf birch

Buxus microphylla 'Kingsville Dwarf'
Kingsville dwarf boxwood

Buxus sempervirens 'Suffruticosa'
True edging boxwood

Cotoneaster microphyllus 'Thymifolius'
Thyme-leaf cotoneaster

Hebe cupressoides 'Boughton Dome'
Boughton dome hebe

Ilex crenata 'Pin Cushion'
Dwarf Japanese holly

Rhododendron impeditum
Cloudland dwarf rhododendron

Rosa 'Si'
Micro-miniature rose

Santolina chamaecyparissus nana
Compact lavender cotton

Ulmus parvifolia 'Hokkaido'
Hokkaido miniature Chinese elm

Little conifers

Abies balsamea 'Nana'
Dwarf balsam fir

Chamaecyparis obtusa 'Nana'
Miniature Hinoki false cypress

Chamaecyparis pisifera 'Boulevard'
Boulevard cypress, Dwarf Sawara cypress

Chamaecyparis thyoides 'Little Jamie'
Dwarf Atlantic white cedar

Juniperus communis 'Compressa'
Dwarf juniper cultivar

Juniperus procumbens 'Nana'
Dwarf Japanese garden juniper

Juniperus squamata 'Blue Star'
Blue star juniper

Picea abies 'Little Gem'
Miniature birdsnest spruce

Picea glauca 'Conica'
Dwarf Alberta spruce

Picea omorika 'Nana'
Dwarf Serbian spruce

Pinus aristata 'Sherwood Compact'
Dwarf bristlecone pine

Pinus mugo 'Valley Cushion'
Dwarf mugho pine cultivar

Thuja occidentalis 'Rheingold'
Rheingold dwarf American arborvitae

Tsuga canadensis 'Cole's Prostrate'
Dwarf weeping Canadian

CHAPTER SEVEN

Building a Garden Railroad

FIG. 7-1. Here's Russ Larson, enjoying running trains on his garden railroad using EDA's radio-controlled, battery-powered system. This lobe of the layout runs around a small pond.

by Russ Larson

My wife, Barb, and I enjoyed garden railroading for eight summers until we sold our house and moved to a condominium. I found that garden railroading complemented rather than competed with my enjoyment of model railroading indoors. Like most midwesterners, I normally don't do much model railroading in the summer. That's the season when we surface from our basements, take in some fresh air and sunshine, and try to forget that after the beautiful fall, winter weather will come once again. Garden railroading extended my model railroad season, so to speak.

The biggest difference between an outdoor layout and an indoor one is that outside, the trains are operating in a real and changing environment. Flowers and plants are growing, and there are insects, birds, and animals living in and on the "layout."

The layout's look and operation can change in just a few minutes if a ground squirrel starts digging near the track or if the wind blows a flower or leaf onto the track. Heavy rains can cause flooding and washouts. A locomotive can lose its footing on wet track. These are conditions unlike any you have to contend with inside, and they make garden railroading exciting and more like prototype conditions.

FIG. 7-2. A freight pulled by an LGB Mogul stops to take on water. That's sedum ground cover in the foreground and silver mound to the right of the water tank.

FIG. 7-3. A Bachmann Big Hauler roars past Bobby's Garage, a structure manufactured by Pola. The tall, brightly colored flowers next to the dwarf mugho pine are feathered cockscombs.

FIG. 7-4. Two of the trains in this photo are being operated by radio control, with the third from track power. The greenery hanging from pockets in the "mountain" is asparagus fern.

FIG. 7-5. An LGB Mogul is pulling a drover's caboose over the cement arch viaduct against a backdrop of petunias. The sedum to the left of the pond is in full bloom. The pond overflow drain can be seen in the foreground.

CONNECTIONS

There used to be a show on PBS called "Connections," which jumped from one subject to the next with some obscure link between them. My interest in garden railways is similarly linked to my first visit to Colorado, which included my introduction to narrow gauge railroading, in 1975; a tour of the LGB factory in 1982; and the introduction of the LGB Mogul in 1985.

Like many model railroaders, I was fascinated by LGB's Mogul and other U.S. prototype Gn3 equipment (and now by other brands as well). I built a quickie outdoor railroad in 1985, more because I wanted a place to run the

FIG. 7-6. A sound-equipped LGB Mogul pulls a "long" freight around the far end loop of the railroad. This section contains a nice selection of the railroad's namesake flowers—impatiens and begonias.

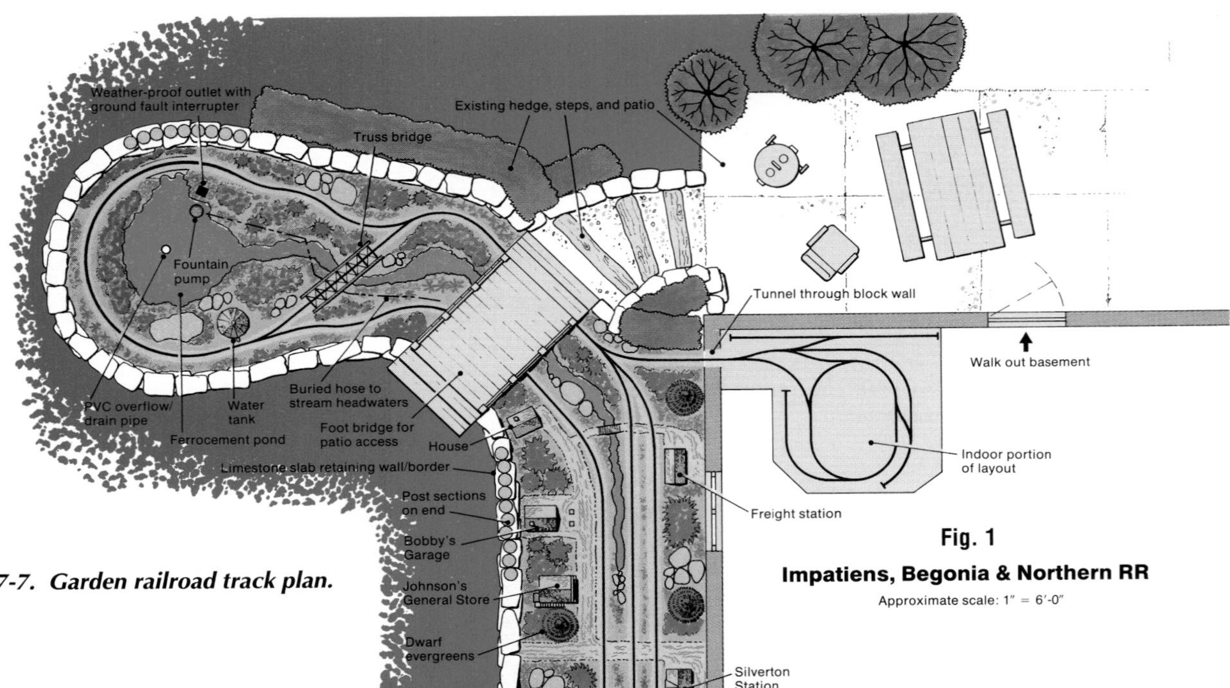

FIG. 7-7. Garden railroad track plan.

equipment I'd accumulated than out of an interest in garden railroading. That first small railroad was built in a weekend, but it was enough to get my wife and me hooked on garden railroading and lead to a much bigger project.

DESIGN CONSIDERATIONS

We began a new garden railroad in the summer of 1988. There were a number of features that we wanted to incorporate. Besides the railroad and garden, we wanted to include structures, artificial scenery, and water. We thought that water would be an important scenic element, and in fact we eventually built two ponds, a running stream, and a waterfall.

All the structures were by Pola. This manufacturer's easy-to-assemble kits are made of a very rugged plastic that holds up well outside. However, to minimize fading from sunlight, we did take them inside during the winter.

Our layout also included some outdoor scenery made from cement—a mountain and one of the two ponds.

TRACK PLAN

The Impatiens, Begonia & Northern, as we named it, was an L-shaped layout. It ran along the back of our house on a route that was approximately 38 feet long and extends about 24 feet from the house. (See **fig. 7-7.**)

Based on my own experience in building a garden railroad, I would suggest that you keep the track plan fairly simple. By simple I mean having a minimum of turnouts. Generally speaking, people build an outdoor railroad because they want to watch the trains run rather than for realistic operation.

By keeping the design simple you are going to minimize maintenance and enhance your enjoyment. An added benefit of a simple plan is reduced construction costs, as the turnouts are quite expensive.

We decided to use LGB's radius 3 curves (117½ cm or 46¼"). The large-radius curves result in smoother operation and give the trains a more realistic appearance as they run.

LGB's line of ready-to-install track and turnouts are sturdy and will stand up to almost all environmental conditions.

And speaking of harsh environments for a garden railroad (people too), we live in southeastern Wisconsin, where the temperature can drop as low as -20 degrees in the winter and rise as high as 100 degrees in the summer.

The indoor connection. The outdoor layout was connected through a "tunnel" chopped in the basement wall to a small indoor layout, which I described in Chapter 4. The main purpose of the indoor layout was equipment storage. It's much easier to run the trains inside under their

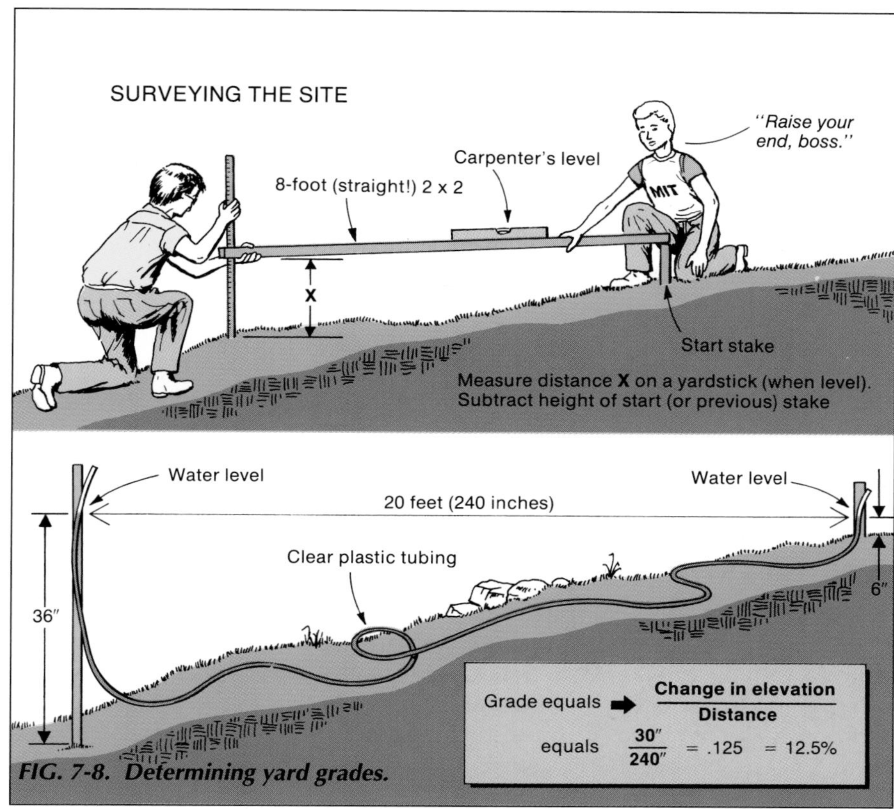

FIG. 7-8. Determining yard grades.

own power than to pick them up and carry them inside after a day's running. It also provided for some limited operation during the cold winter months.

On the indoor portion of the layout, we used LGB's radius 1 (60 cm or 23⅝") and radius 2 (76½ cm or 30") curves due to space limitations.

SURVEYING THE SITE

Garden railroading is very much like prototype railroading when it comes to surveying and grading the right-of-way. The first step is to get the lay of the land to see how steep the grades are going to be and where culverts, bridges, and trestles will be needed for natural drainage.

Depending on the slope of your property, you may have to do some cutting and filling to reduce the natural grade, just like real railroads do when a new line is built.

Our home at that time was built on a sloping lot—sloping enough that one side of our basement is exposed. I determined that our lot slopes about 2 feet in the 40-foot span between the end lobes of the proposed L-shaped layout. Without any additional landscaping, that would have resulted in a grade of about 5 percent, which I felt was much too steep. So I decided to fill the northwest lobe of the railroad to a height of about 1 foot above the existing grade and cut the other lobe down about 4". The result was a maximum grade of about 2½ percent, which proved to be quite acceptable.

My method of determining the slope of the yard was to use a carpenter's level and a straight 8-foot length of 2 x 2. As shown in **fig. 7-8,** we (it takes two people) started at the highest area of the yard and worked our way across, noting the drop in each 8 feet.

An 8-foot stick is 96" long, very close to 100". That helps, because when you measure the slope of the yard in inches you automatically get the grade's percent. In other words, a 4" drop in 100" is a downgrade of 4 percent.

My crude method worked quite well for our landscaped lot with its gradual slope. A better method, and one that's a must for ungraded property, is to determine the grade using a water level. (See **fig. 7-8.**) Commercial water levels and inexpensive plastic tubing are sold in hardware stores.

As alternatives you could rent surveying equipment or have it done professionally.

BULLWORK

After surveying the site, we assembled the LGB track into the planned configuration to see how it fit and where retaining walls were necessary on the end to be elevated. The sod was removed from this area, and we prepared to install limestone retaining walls.

We chose limestone for two reasons. First, it's a common stone that's quarried locally and is relatively inexpensive. Second, our flower garden and some other retaining walls around the house are built of the same stone.

Limestone roughly cut into slabs for retaining walls is sold by the ton. We used 3 tons for edging the garden railroad. The pieces are heavy and have to be selected for appearance and fit. This means repeated handling of each piece. Fortunately, my son helped with the retaining wall construction. (See **fig. 7-9.**)

The rough excavation work for the cement stream and pond (construction will be described later) was done after we had the limestone retaining wall in place.

ROADBED

One of the first questions new garden railroad builders ask is, "What type of roadbed is best?" Based on articles I read in *Garden Railways,* I determined that the "floating" method was best for northern climates like ours. With this method you let the track float on a bed of stone; that way it's unaffected by frost upheavals. (In less hostile environments other roadbed methods have been successful. See Chapter 6.)

The floating roadbed worked very well. We had no problems through a number of harsh Wisconsin winters. As with prototype roadbed, the stone provides a stable base for the track and good drainage.

Where the right-of-way goes through stable soil, you need only dig a trench about 8" wide and fill it with crushed stone. Where the roadbed passes above the existing grade of the yard, it's necessary to build a trough for the roadbed and then fill in dirt on both sides. I made the trough out of plastic lawn edging nailed to 2 x 2 stakes (**fig. 7-10**).

After assembling the track, I marked its center line and the locations for the trough stakes. Then I disassembled the track and began working in earnest on the roadbed.

Even though you have done the rough surveying, it's still a good idea to check the level of the trough as it's being installed. I found that a 2-foot level worked quite well to give me a good idea of the grade. (See **fig. 7-11.**) A 1" rise in 25" equals a grade of 4 percent, so a half-inch rise in the 2-foot length of the level is a bit more than a 2 percent grade, which is what I wanted.

It's also important to check that the trough sides are level so the track will lie flat. On curves a very slight rise to the outside (superelevation) is okay.

Once I'd finished the trough, I filled it with crushed limestone. It then took 5 yards of topsoil to bring the "garden" up to the level of the roadbed.

UNDERGROUND WIRING

Our wiring is quite simple. The layout is wired for operating one train from track power. We operate other trains from batteries and use radio control. Wiring an outdoor layout presents special challenges, particularly if the layout is being built at ground level. The wires must be buried in the ground and are definitely not readily accessible. I did bundle the wires so that if we had to get at them later they would have been easier to locate.

We have a hose running from the cement pond to the stream to recycle water. I taped the bundled wires to the hose, as shown in **fig. 7-12.**

We made electrical connections to the track in four places—one each on the outermost lobes and two equally spaced intermediate connections. (If I were to build a new garden railroad, I would use radio control of battery-powered trains and eliminate track wiring.)

Our layout did have a reverse loop, which required gaps and extra wiring. In addition to the reverse loop, the layout had one passing siding. Power to the siding could be cut, so an engine could be stored there while another one runs on the rest of the layout.

FIG. 7-9. The author's son Craig was a big help when it came to building the limestone retaining walls. The heavy, rough-cut slabs must be handled repeatedly to get a good fit. Lines strung between the stakes ensured that the flower bed would be level.

FIG. 7-10. Above: The author used plastic lawn edging nailed to 2 x 2 stakes to form a roadbed trough. He called Diggers Hotline before digging. Flags mark the route of buried electric lines. Right: The trough was filled with crushed limestone.

FIG. 7-11. Above: It's important to make sure the trough sides are level so the track will lie flat. Left: The author makes a final check of the track to be sure the grade does not exceed 2 percent.

In addition to the track wiring, two wires were run from each of the five switch machines, which operate on 18 volts DC, to the control box.

CONTROL BOX AND POWER

I used miniature switches and mounted them in a utility box. There's one double-pole, double throw (DPDT) switch for the reversing loop and another for the main line. A single-pole, single-throw (SPST) switch takes care of the siding. LGB offers a complete line of wiring accessories, including control boxes for turnout control, but I chose to use miniature DPDT,

FIG. 7-12. Wiring an outdoor railroad presents some new challenges because the wiring is underground. The author bundled the wires together whenever possible. Here he tapes wires to the hose that recycles pond water.

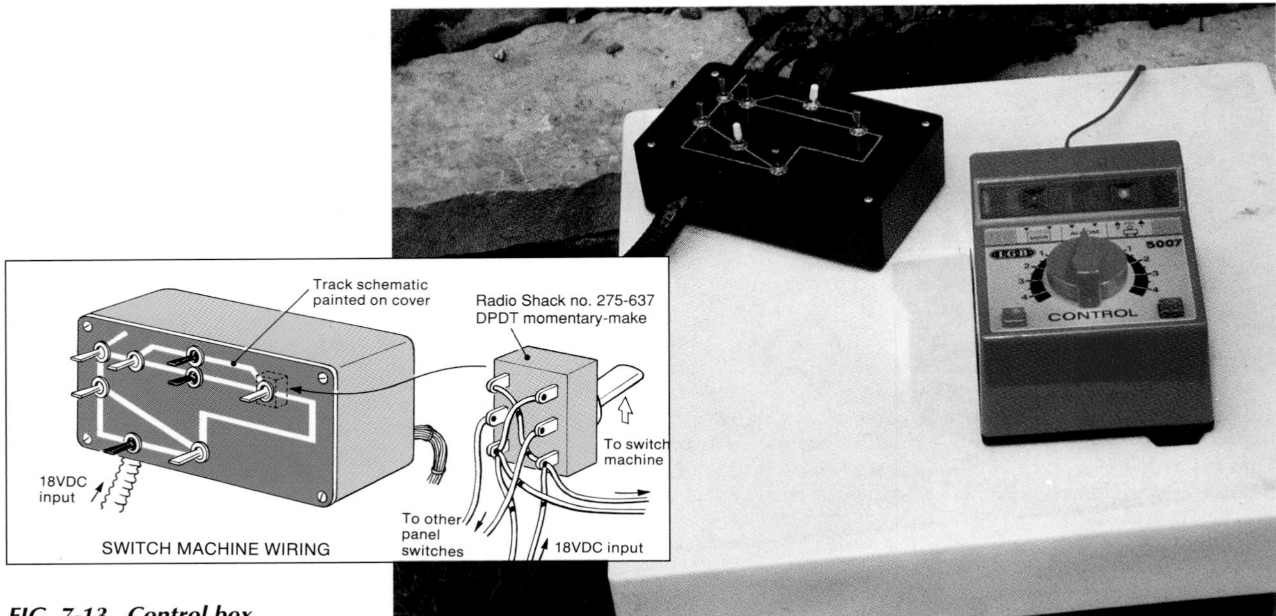

FIG. 7-13. Control box.

momentary-make switches instead. All switches were mounted in position on a schematic of the layout on the aluminum cover of the utility box. (See **fig. 7-13.**)

An LGB transformer (item no. 5006) and electronic speed controller (no. 5007) were used for train and turnout power. I followed LGB's safety advice and installed the transformer inside the house and ran only the low-voltage wiring outside to operate the electronic speed controller and the turnouts.

TRACKLAYING

The biggest problem you have with operating trains from track power outside is corrosion and dirt in the rail joints. These significantly reduce the electrical conductivity. Handy devices that solve this problem are Bond'R Clamps, made by John Row. (Other firms offer similar clamps.) These clamps are installed over each rail joint; when tightened, they squeeze the joint tightly to form a good electrical and mechanical connection, as shown in **fig. 7-14.**

There are other, less expensive ways to eliminate this problem. One method is to solder jumper wires around each joint, using a small torch. The brass rail has to be thoroughly cleaned at each connection point, and you have to use a noncorrosive flux. It's tricky, but it can be done. Another way is to drill and tap holes through the rail joiner and into the rail on each side. Install screws, and you'll have joints that are both mechanically and electrically sound.

LGB now offers 1½-meter (approximately 5-foot) lengths of flexible track. If I were starting now, I'd use these to reduce the number of rail joints. Also, Micro Engineering offers 6-foot lengths of aluminum rail that can be inserted into the LGB tie strips.

BALLASTING

Initially I tried using pea gravel for ballast. Though it worked fine, it didn't look good because it's much too large. Later I learned that chicken grit makes a good ballast. It's crushed granite and is offered in several sizes. I like the small size intended for young chicks and called "starter grit." A comparison of pea gravel and chicken grit as ballast is shown in **figs. 7-15** and **7-16.** In most places no adhesive is needed to hold the ballast in place. Where the ballast slope is steep, you may have to use cement adhesive to secure it.

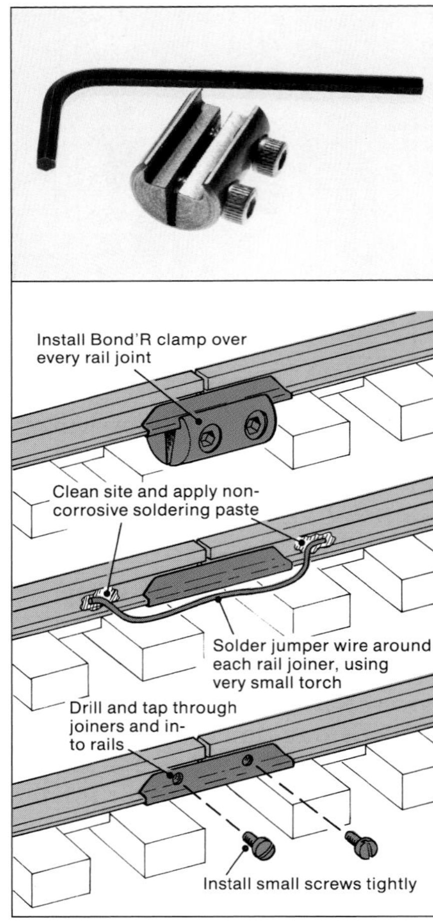

FIG. 7-14. Eliminating problems in rail joints.

FIG. 7-15. Pea gravel works all right for ballast, but it's too big to look realistic.

SCENERY

Scenery on a garden railroad can consist entirely of natural elements. Dirt, rocks, bark, trees, shrubs, ground cover, and flowers all look good. However, it's also possible to introduce some artificial elements such as structures, vehicles, people, ponds, and artificial rocks.

There have been many books written on gardening, landscaping, and water gardening. Check your local public library or garden supply center. As with any new endeavor, it's best to study the subject before plunging in.

While I was looking for a way to make a pond, I stumbled across a book at the public library called *Ferrocement*, by Stanley Abercrombie. Ferrocement is steel-reinforced concrete on a small scale. The steel adds strength to the cement and expands and contracts at the same rate. Basically, you trowel mortar onto an overlapping mesh of chicken wire, as shown in **fig. 7-17.** The result is a thin shell of cement that is very strong—very much like the hardshell scenery that is used for building indoor model railroads.

A key step in getting good-quality ferrocement is the curing process. It's important for the finished cement work to be wetted several times a day for about a week.

STREAMS AND PONDS

We had two ponds in the garden. One was made of ferrocement,

FIG. 7-16. Chicken grit, available in feed stores, looks much better. It's crushed granite that's available in several sizes. The author likes "starter grit."

while the other was formed by sheet rubber. We've dubbed the second the "rubber pond."

An important consideration when designing a pond is drainage. We get heavy summer rains, and without some kind of overflow the pond would flood the adjoining flower beds and wash them away.

Fortunately, the natural slope of the land in the area of our rubber pond was such that the overflow runs harmlessly onto the lawn.

However, if the cement pond didn't have an overflow pipe, garden flooding would have resulted. To prevent flood damage I installed a drain and overflow system made of PVC pipe. (See **fig. 7-18.**)

While the cement pond worked out well and looked nice, it was a real effort to build. Building the rubber pond was faster and easier, and it looked almost as good. (See **fig. 7-19.**) There are also preformed plastic ponds and troughs available at garden supply centers.

We used one fountain pump to recycle the water from the cement pond back to the headwaters of the

FIG. 7-17. Above: The first step in the ferrocement process is to install overlapping layers of chicken wire. Right: Mortar is troweled into the wire mesh. Below: The ferrocement stream was completed and the work on the pond was about half done when this photo was taken.

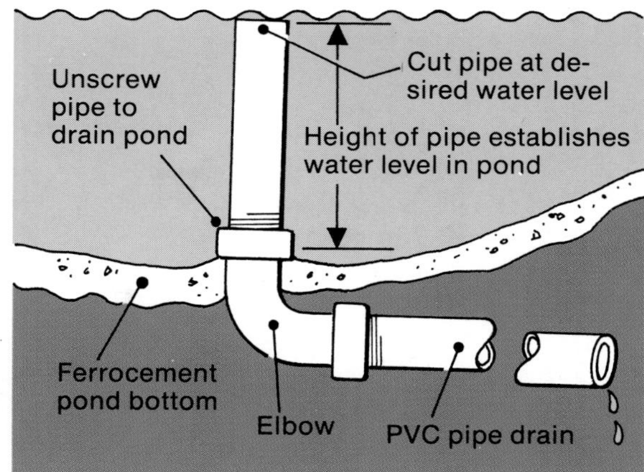

FIG. 7-18. Left: A PVC drain pipe was installed prior to the cement work. The end cap on the elbow was not used. Right: The drawing shows how the drain and overflow system was built and how it works.

stream. Another was placed in the rubber pond to pump water to the top of our "mountain," where it cascaded down into two small basins formed in the cement and then tumbled back into the pond.

The water in the ponds and flowing in the stream and down the mountainside added peaceful sights and sounds to the garden. The ponds were also home to goldfish. Visitors enjoyed discovering them, and they had a practical benefit—they fed on mosquito larvae.

Safety. While these small, submersible fountain pumps, sold at garden supply centers, are generally safe to use, it is advisable to follow standard safety precautions, including the use of outlets with ground fault interrupters.

FIG 7-19. Left: The ferrocement "mountain" was placed so it would cover the sump pump discharge hose and the gutter downspout. Below: A flimsy framework for the "mountain" was built of 1 x 2s. Plastic wastebaskets were cemented together for tunnel lines. The pond in the foreground was quickly made using a heavy sheet of rubber, the type used for roofs. The edges were lined with stones to hold the rubber in place. The natural slope of the yard is toward the lawn, making a drain unnecessary.

THE "MOUNTAIN"

The back of our home was fairly typical of those in our area in that some of the necessary utilities were located there, such as the electric power meter, the sump pump discharge, and one of the gutter downspouts. We wanted to have a "mountain" with tunnels through it and decided to place the mountain where it would cover up these unsightly utilities.

Unfortunately, we couldn't hide the electric company's meter, but we did manage to hide the sump discharge and the downspout.

CHAPTER EIGHT

Large Scale Showcase

These 16-foot-high mountains represent just a small part of the huge Gn3 layout that fills the 35 x 75-foot lobby at the Children's Medical Center of Dallas, Texas. Photo by Malcom Furlow.

A passenger train passes a freight waiting in the station on Dennis Johnson's Johnson Pass Spur in Colorado. The vertical landscape timbers form a retaining wall that elevates the railway to a convenient height and provides a visual separation between the railway and the lawn. The diesel locomotive is by LGB and the steamer by Lionel. Photo by Richard Schafer.

Train time at Hawk Creek on Robert Barton's line in England. The station is a heavily modified and weathered Playmobil structure. Engine and rolling stock are by LGB. We are right down on the track in this photo, skillfully shot by the line's owner.

A double-headed mixed train passes over the high bridge on Charles Grant's Georgetown Loop RR in Colorado; a freight train passes beneath. This line was built into an existing high-altitude landscape of native plants. Garden lines operate all year round, as this snow shot suggests. Photo by Marc Horovitz.

Natural-looking rock placement and plant material bring Dick Schafer's Galena Railway & Navigation Company to life. The rolling stock is a mixture of LGB, Delton, Bachmann, scratchbuilt, and other commercially available kits. Track floats in ballast, which allows it to expand and contract with changing weather conditions. A carpet of blue-flowering Turkish veronica (Veronica liwanensis) lights up the foreground. Photo by Barbara Horovitz.

No. 3, a modified LGB engine, takes a passenger train out of the station at El Patio on Herb Chaudiere's Cranis Garden Railway in Washington State. Structures are a mixture of commercial products and scratchbuilt. Trains on the Cranis have full sound systems and are run by radio control. Photo by Herb Chaudiere.

Colorado & Southern no. 22 pauses at Jefferson tank. Joe Crea built the engine on an LGB chassis for a European prototype locomotive. The basic materials were acrylic tube, brass, and sheet styrene. He made the tender by laminating sheet styrene to a wood block. The unique C&S spark arrestor was fabricated from a sheet of brass and has working hinges. Photo by Terry Metcalfe.

Produce is unloaded from the reefer stopped at Lomita Junction on Steve & Judy Arrigotti's Mother Lode line in Northern California. The owners have created many such engaging vignettes from miniatures, structures, and rolling stock nestled into the landscape. Photo by Steve Arrigotti.

Trolley lines are still not modeled much outdoors, though streetcars are offered in G scale by both LGB and Bachmann. Here a street railway exists on a dirt main street on Fran and Carl Pfetzing's intricate line in Southern California. Notice the carefully selected flora used to complement the setting. Photo by Marc Horovitz.

Union Pacific in 1:32 scale. A train headed by a pair of Lionel GP-20s passes a freight pulled by an F9 A-B lashup from Chicago Train Works on David & Marily Charles' Denver & Rio Ondo garden line in Colorado. As large scale becomes more popular, it's getting easier to create railroads featuring modern era diesel engines. Photo by Marc Horovitz.

A Roberts' Line 1:32 scale Burlington Zephyr crosses an all-metal deck girder bridge on David & Marily Charles' Denver & Rio Ondo line in Colorado. Photo by Marc Horovitz.

CHAPTER NINE

Introduction to Live Steam

*FIG. 9-1. Live steam reigns on the South Pacific Coast, Grover Devine's line in California's Bay Area. These are modified Merlin locomotives, made in Great Britain. Steam emerging from the smokestacks is 100% natural—nothing has been done to enhance the effect or create artificial smoke. The conifers are dwarf Alberta spruce (*Picea glauca *'Conica').*

by Marc Horovitz

Operating your own live-steam locomotive is one of the ultimate thrills in model railroading. In North America, this experience has been limited to the few modelers willing to spend many years constructing something that was big enough to ride around on, or to those who had enough money to buy a ready-made locomotive. Membership in a club (with a running track) or an enormous backyard was also a prerequisite to live-steam operation.

In the past few years, though, things have changed, and a new face has appeared in the crowd of model railroading alternatives—small scale live steam. However, the "small scale" designation in live steam is different from the usual modelers' use of the term to mean N or Z scale. In live steam, "small scale" usually refers to models in the ½" to ¼" scale range. O scale seems to be about the smallest practical size for live-steam operation, although there have been successful experimental models in even smaller scales. In this country, gauge 1 is the most popular gauge for little steam engines. A small scale live-steam locomotive may be defined as any steam-powered locomotive between ¼" and 1" scale that is not intended to carry passengers. While some live steamers may be run in perfect safety and with great success indoors, they are primarily used outdoors in the garden.

HISTORY

Small scale live steam is not a new phenomenon—steam-operated model trains predate electric trains by many years. The history of toy and model trains is well documented, so it is sufficient to say that model steam engines developed along with the prototypes up until World War II. After the war people lost interest in the larger scales in general and live steam in particular.

In the late 1940s and early 1950s, the trend was toward miniaturization. Lionel, the recognized O gauge leader in the world of toy and model trains, experienced a regular decline in sales after a peak in the mid-1950s. HO, and later N, skyrocketed into popularity. Gauge 1 railroading, never popular in this country anyway, became a dimly remembered relic of the past.

In England, things developed in a somewhat different direction. Bassett-Lowke, the great British model train manufacturer, continued to make live-steam engines for a while into the 1950s. During this period of low interest, a small fraction of modelers continued to use gauge 1 for their steam, clockwork, and electric models.

Hobbyists had always looked upon commercial steam locomotives as good performers—on bright sunny days, on straight and level track. If any of these conditions varied, you were on your own. It must be admitted that there was some basis for this thinking. Of course, there have always been some scratchbuilt models that ran well, so people knew that it was possible to get good operation from miniature steam engines.

In the 1960s, small scale steam modeling got a shot in the arm when Stewart Browne, an Englishman, started a company called Archangel Models. Browne believed that he could make—on a production basis—small scale live-steam locomotives that were easy to control, would run unassisted for a reasonable length of time, and would operate at realistic speeds.

Working with 16 mm-to-the-foot scale (slightly larger than ½" scale), Browne began building models of British and Welsh 2-foot narrow gauge locomotives, which ran on O gauge track. His results were impressive, and they were the beginning of the renaissance of small scale steam locomotives.

LIVE STEAM TODAY

As you may have gathered, Great Britain is the world capital of small scale live steam. There are at least half a dozen small British companies whose sole business is manufacturing small scale live steamers. Small steam engines are also produced in Germany, Switzerland, France, Australia, Japan, Canada, and the United States.

Aster of Japan is probably the firm most responsible for bringing small scale steam to world attention. This Japanese builder has produced a whole fleet of beautiful locomotives that range in sophistication from a single-oscillating-cylindered, British outline 0-6-0T to an exceedingly sophisticated Union Pacific Big Boy 4-8-8-4 fired by coal or gas (your choice). When produced, this articulated sported full working Walschaerts valve gear, 60 psi working pressure, two safety valves, blower, pressure gauge, water glass, blowdown valve, whistle, and a price tag of around $10,000. Obviously, this engine is not for everyone.

Many people assume that a live-steam locomotive is vastly more expensive than an electric engine, and that live steam is one of the last strongholds of the very rich. Nothing could be further from the truth. Modelers working with a relatively small budget can have a lot of fun with steam, too. What is true is that if you have two models of the same prototype, in the same scale, built to an equal degree of craftsmanship, one electric and one live steam, the live-steam engine will cost more.

A live-steam locomotive is more expensive because its manufacturing process is labor-intensive. Boilers have to be constructed and tested to at least twice their working pressure, cylinders must be perfectly smooth and true on the inside, pistons must be fitted accurately, and fittings must be functional and efficient—all of this takes time and, as you may have heard, time is money.

However, the blanket statement that steam engines cost more than electric engines isn't true. There are live steamers on the market for under $500. The Mamod company of Great Britain, before it went out of business, produced thousands of 0-4-0T locomotives in gauges 0 and 1 for under $200. These often turn up on the second-hand market, and often constitute a good buy.

STEAM ENGINE THEORY

I have met modelers who declaim at length that they are steam fanatics and that any diesel caught trespassing on their railroads will be shot on sight. This is not necessarily bad in itself. When pressed, though, this same set often reveals that they haven't the foggiest notion of how a steam engine actually works. For their benefit and for anyone else unfamiliar with real steam engines, let's take a closer look at the process. (See **fig. 9-2.**)

In its most basic form, a steam engine is little more than a piston (much like an automobile piston) that is moved in a cylinder by the pressure of steam. (See **fig. 9-3.**) The cylinder may be single-acting, meaning that the piston is shoved in one direction only and relies on the kinetic energy stored in a flywheel

Operating System of Model Live-Steam Locomotives
Steam dome
Smokestack
Superheater
Steam line
Throttle
Smoke box
Fuel control
To cylinders
Fire-
box
Exhaust
Fuel
tank
Steam chest
Cylinder
Sump
Fuel line
Wick tubes
Fire tubes
Valve gear

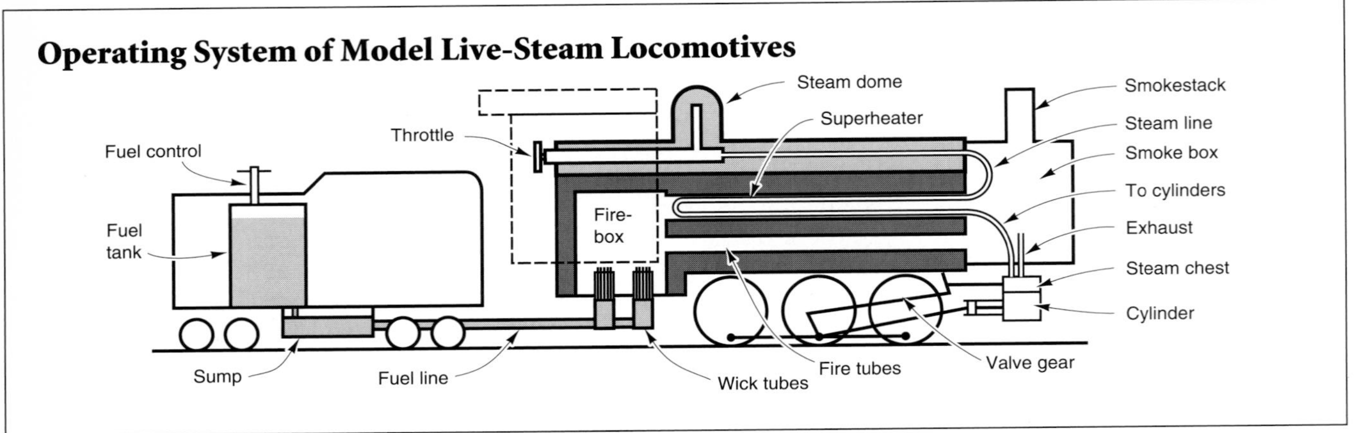

FIG. 9-2. Cutaway of a small scale live steamer showing all the main components.

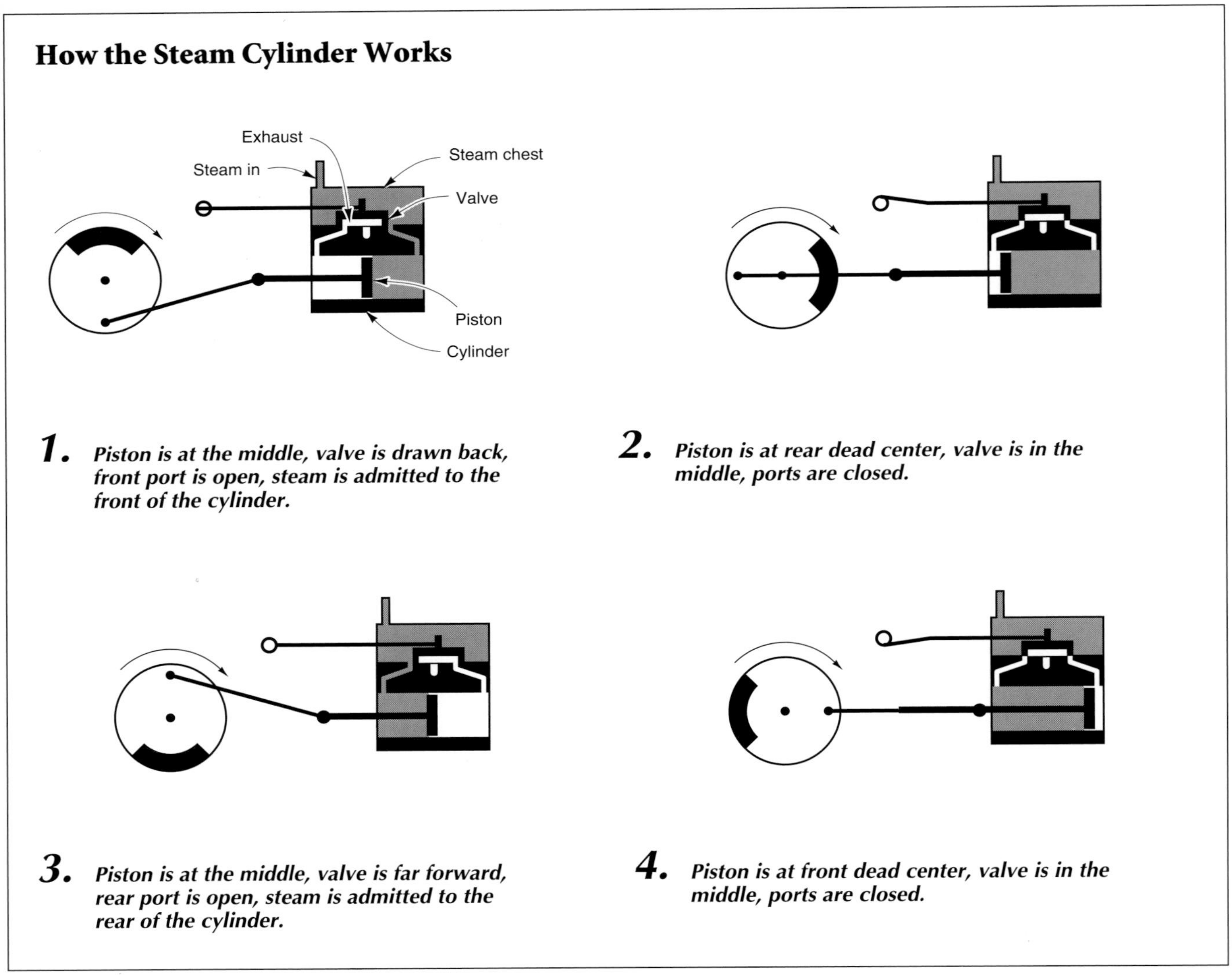

How the Steam Cylinder Works
Exhaust
Steam in
Steam chest
Valve
Piston
Cylinder
1. Piston is at the middle, valve is drawn back, front port is open, steam is admitted to the front of the cylinder.
2. Piston is at rear dead center, valve is in the middle, ports are closed.
3. Piston is at the middle, valve is far forward, rear port is open, steam is admitted to the rear of the cylinder.
4. Piston is at front dead center, valve is in the middle, ports are closed.

FIG. 9-3. This series of drawings shows how the power of steam is converted to rotary motion.

to return it to its original position; or it may be double-acting, meaning that the piston is pushed back and forth by alternately admitting steam into opposite ends of the cylinder.

The device that admits steam to the cylinder and exhausts steam from it is called the valve. There are several different types of valves; they are fully covered in technical books on steam and need not be extensively explored here. Basically, the valve moves back and forth, covering and uncovering holes or ports that admit steam to the cylinders and allow the exhaust to escape so that the piston may return. This must be done with precision, so the valve must be accurately controlled.

The device that controls the valve is called the valve gear. The valve gear can be as simple as an eccentric on the driven axle, or as complex as one of the full-size locomotive valve gears, such as Stephenson's Link or Walschaerts. All valve gears perform the same function in different ways, admitting and releasing steam from the cylinders with a greater or lesser degree of efficiency.

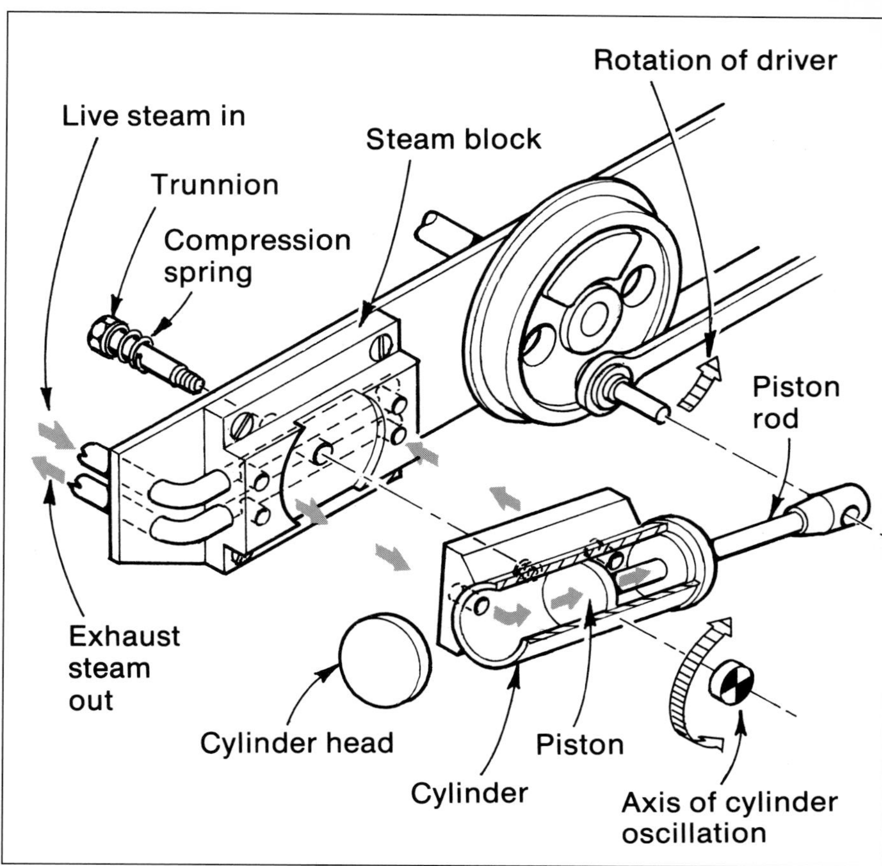

FIG. 9-4. Double-acting oscillating cylinder.

There is, however, an extremely simple cylinder that requires no valve at all. This is the oscillating cylinder, shown in **fig. 9-4,** which saw limited use on full-size locomotives. An oscillator may be single- or double-acting. This is how it works: The cylinder is mounted to a flat block that pivots on a trunnion placed halfway down its length. The flat face of the cylinder block bears against a steam block. The trunnion penetrates the steam block and is held in place by a spring that binds the cylinder to the steam block while still allowing it to rotate.

A hole is made in the flat face of the cylinder at each end to admit and exhaust steam. The piston rod is attached directly to the wheel. As the wheel turns, the piston and cylinder are forced to oscillate up and down. At the top and bottom of the wheel's revolution, the cylinder is at the two extreme positions. There are four holes made in the steam block, two each to mate with the holes in the cylinder at each of its extreme positions. They are the admission and exhaust ports. All you have to do is apply steam to either of the ports to make the engine run. If the engine is going the wrong way, simply reverse the admission and exhaust and you have reversed the engine.

To make the steam for the cylinders, you need a boiler. A locomotive boiler must not only be functional, but must be designed for the specific engine that it is mounted on. There are dozens of boiler designs and variations, but they all fall into two basic categories—externally fired and internally fired. An externally fired boiler (also called a "pot boiler") is just that. The fire is entirely outside the boiler. An internally fired boiler has tubes running through it that carry hot gases on their way from the fire to the smokebox and stack. These tubes increase the surface area (or heating area) of the boiler and make it more efficient. However, the tubes cut down the water capacity of the boiler, which is an important consideration in small scale steam.

One way to increase both surface area and water capacity is to extend tubes full of water down from the boiler into the fire. Unfortunately, designs like this decrease the fire space. A good boiler is a delicate balance of many factors. Most of the commercially available locomotives have well-designed boilers.

Steam is transported from the boiler to the cylinders through a steam pipe or line. The amount of steam is controlled by a sensitive valve, commonly known as the throttle. Depending upon the sophistication of the model, the boiler may have fittings on it to help run the engine or provide information to the engineer about the state of the boiler.

Many of the other fittings are

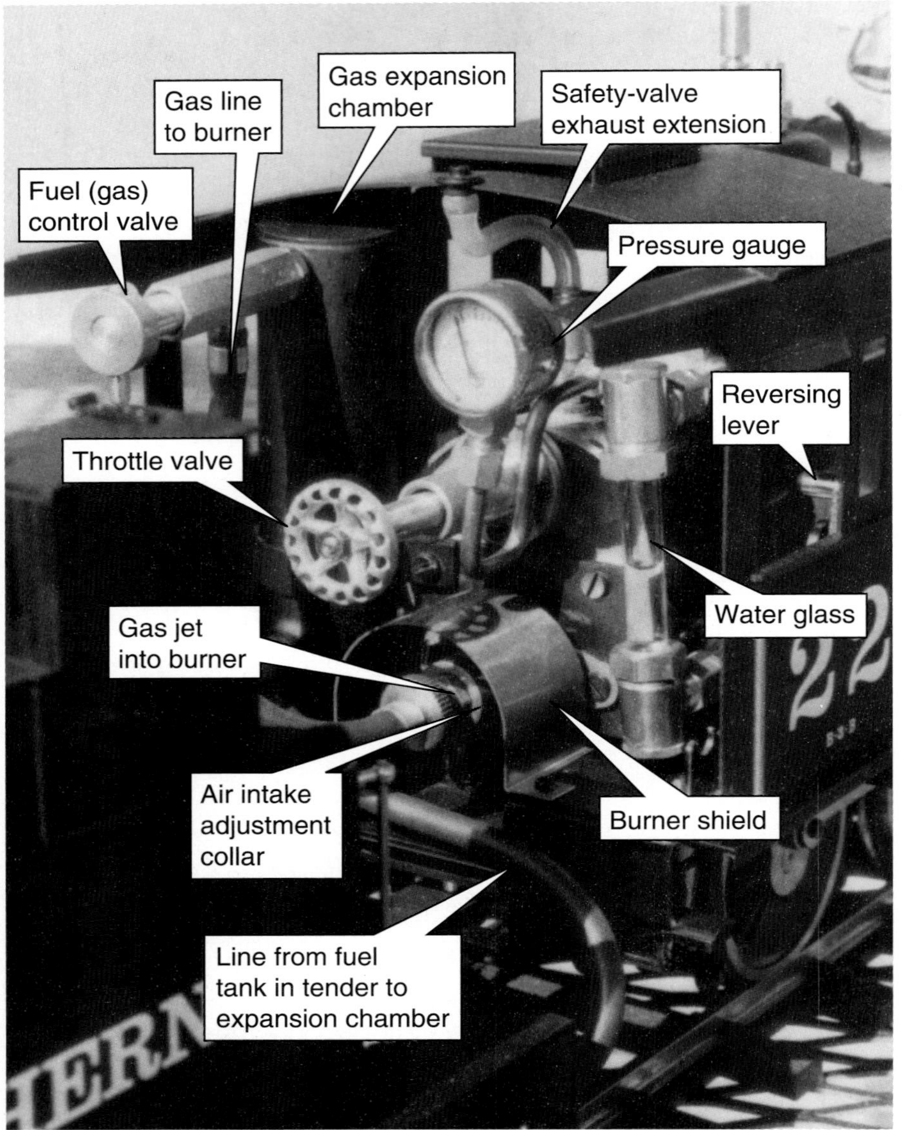

FIG. 9-5. ***Many controls on small scale live-steam engines serve the same purpose as those on full-scale locomotives. An Aster gauge 1 Colorado & Southern 2-6-0 is pictured here.***

miniature versions of controls found on full-scale locomotives. These fittings, shown in **fig. 9-5,** may or may not be found on a specific model locomotive. The blower valve controls a jet of steam released up the stack to create a partial vacuum that pulls the fire and heat through an internally fired boiler. A reversing lever may be used if the locomotive is sophisticated enough to have working valve gear. A pressure gauge tells the engineer if steam is up or down and can give an indication of the state of the fire, which is not always visible. A water glass helps the engineer keep track of the amount of water in the boiler. Some engines have a blowdown valve, which allows the engineer to safely discharge the remaining steam from the boiler at the end of the run.

Every steam locomotive must also have at least one functional safety valve. This is an automatic valve set on the boiler that releases excess steam pressure. A boiler is normally tested to at least twice its working pressure, so this valve maintains a large margin of safety. Never tamper with the safety valve, unless you are extremely knowledgeable about steam matters and know precisely what you are doing.

OPERATION

One of the joys of small scale steam is getting to know your locomotive. Every engine has its very own personality, and it takes some practice to get the best performance out of any given engine. This quality has the tendency to bring the engines to life—to make them personal machines.

A live-steam locomotive is not as difficult to operate as one might imagine, particularly in these smaller sizes. On a full-size locomotive, the operator must watch the water lever, the state of the fire, the boiler pressure, and several other things. Many small engines are designed so that the boiler and fuel reservoirs may be filled and left alone until the end of the run. The fire is usually designed to go out before the boiler is empty, to prevent damage to the boiler. Thus, the engineer's greatest concern is the speed of the train, which is easily regulated by adjusting the throttle.

Let's pretend you're the engineer for a day's run with a live-steam locomotive. A typical operating session begins at the steaming bay (a short length of track used only for raising steam), or you may raise steam on a bench or on the mainline. First, examine the engine carefully to make sure that everything is in good working order. Try moving all of the controls to ensure that they are not frozen. Lift the safety valve manually to make sure it isn't stuck. Next, oil all of the moving parts—crank pins, axles, cross heads, etc. This oiling must be done before every run.

After you finish the inspection, fill the boiler with distilled water, as shown in **fig. 9-6.** You may do this through a filler plug, or you may choose to pump the water in through a pump built into the engine or at trackside. Carefully watch the water level coming up in the water glass to keep from overfilling the boiler. When the boiler is

FIG. 9-6. John Carlson fires up his modified Aster 0-4-2T live steamer on the raised portion of Grover Devine's South Pacific Coast Railway in California. All track is handlaid on this line. The miniature pomegranate tree is actually in a pot that is inset into the benchwork.

filled to the proper level, add steam oil to the engine's lubricator. Steam oil is a special, very viscous oil formulated for use in steam cylinders. Don't use regular machine oil; it tends to disappear immediately under the conditions found inside the cylinder. Fill the alcohol tank and then open the valve to the burner. You're now ready to light the fire.

On more sophisticated engines, a suction fan—usually battery powered—is necessary to pull the fire through the boiler to raise steam. If your engine needs the fan, insert it in the smokestack and turn it on. Light the fire with a long match, and then use a dentist's mirror to see that all of the wicks are burning. At this point you can feel the heat coming through the fan. After four or five minutes the pressure gauge will read about 15 pounds per square inch.

While 15 psi is not enough pressure to run the engine, it is enough to run the engine's own blower and dispense with the electric fan. Go easy when you open the blower valve, as it usually allows a little hot water to spit out of the stack and blow through the fan. When the blower line is clear and a steady stream of steam is shooting up the stack, the auxiliary fan is no longer necessary, so you may remove it. Once the blower is running, the pressure comes up at a faster rate until the engine reaches the working pressure of 45 psi. A continued increase in the pressure will cause the safety valve to release a plume of white steam.

On your initial run of the day, cracking the throttle will start the flow of steam to the cylinders. However, the cylinders are cold at this point, so the engine must be pushed along the track to clear the condensate and heat the cylinders. Once they are warm, you may open the throttle, turn off the blower, and let the train move smoothly out onto the main line to begin its journey. As the engine passes, check the steam pressure and boiler water level, and make the necessary minor control adjustments.

A typical run may last about half an hour or so. Then you refuel and water the engine and make it ready for the next run. At the end of the day, allow the locomotive to cool and then wipe it down with a damp rag. Make another inspection to look for damage or loose parts, and siphon off any water that is present in the lubricator. Finally, drain the boiler so that the engine can be stored, ready for the next running session.

Running a live-steam locomotive is definitely a hands-on affair, but that is part of the philosophy and charm of live steam. These are real steam locomotives in miniature and must be treated as such.

RADIO CONTROL

Controlling small scale, live-steam engines has traditionally been a matter of being in the right place at the right time to adjust the controls manually as conditions warrant. Radio control has changed this. Some locomotive manufacturers now offer radio control as a factory-added option, or design

FIG. 9-7. An Americanized Roundhouse Engineering live-steam 0-4-0 takes a train across the lower track on Dutton Foster's PD&Q in Minnesota. Note the rustic cribbing to the left of the scratchbuilt wood tunnel portal. Phloxes provide spring color on the line.

their engines so that radios may be easily added later. Even a single-channel radio controlling the throttle makes a world of difference. With an additional reverse control, a live-steam engine is easily able to perform the most complex switching operations without having to be touched. Thus we can achieve the best of both worlds: the ease of operation of electric trains (without the wires) and the satisfaction of live steam.

GETTING STARTED

Getting started in live steam may be a bit difficult, primarily because few train shops in the United States stock these engines or have any knowledge of the subject. Perhaps the best way to get started is to read the specialty magazines, like *Garden Railways* or *Steam in the Garden,* and respond to the ads in them. Most of the suppliers are happy to answer questions about their products. As time goes on and this aspect of the hobby becomes more and more popular, I'm certain that ads for small scale steam will appear in the larger, more mainstream publications as well.

Once you make the decision to get into live steam, your next most important decision is choosing your first steam locomotive. Here are a few points to consider:

Experience. Do you have any experience, either actual or vicarious, with any aspect of live steam, or are you starting out cold, so to speak? If you have no practical experience (many new small scale, live-steam modelers don't), it is important that your first steam experience be a good one. I've heard many tales of people buying locomotives that were too sophisticated or complicated for them. They were not able to get the engines to run properly and were eventually discouraged.

For your first engine, choose a simple but proven locomotive like the Mamod engine from England. This engine's solid fuel burner is not altogether adequate; but two or three companies offer alcohol or gas (butane) burners designed specifically for the Mamod engines that transform them from a timid, halting toy into a useful and strong-running locomotive.

Kits vs. ready-to-run. If you are mechanically inclined, you may wish to purchase a kit. One advantage to assembling a kit is that it gives you the opportunity to learn just how a steam engine functions.

Two manufacturers have offered ready-to-assemble kits—Mamod of England and Aster of Japan. Mamod has not been producing locomotives for some years now, and the disposition of the company is still in question. However, the company's kits still turn up occasionally.

Nearly all Aster locomotives are sophisticated scale models that take many hours of careful work to assemble. (See **fig. 9-8.**) I normally do not recommend an Aster engine as a first locomotive, although many people have had great success with them on the first go-round. Their valve gears require adjusting just as those of full-size locomotives do, and this is sometimes difficult and frustrating if you do not fully understand what is supposed to happen.

Mamod kits, on the other hand, are simple to assemble in just a few hours. Mamod has sacrificed detail and sophistication for simplicity.

FIG. 9-8. Steam locomotive kits may require many hours of assembly. Here you see the numerous pieces of an Aster live-steam Climax.

Both Aster and Mamod kits are prepainted. Both feature true screwdriver assembly, requiring no machine work or soldering.

Most ready-to-run locomotives in my experience have been factory tested, so you are reasonably assured of getting a good product. It never hurts, however, to do a little research work.

Obtain and carefully read the manufacturer's specifications. If you can, talk to someone who has had personal experience with the locomotive before you make your purchase. Live-steam engines vary widely in their characteristics and performance qualities.

Expense. Generally speaking, lower-priced engines are simpler, and higher-priced engines are more complex. If you are just getting started, a lower-cost simple engine is usually preferable.

Operation. What do you want from your locomotive? Do you want to be able to sit on your back-porch swing for half an hour at a time and watch the train as it trundles through your garden? Or do you want more active involvement with your locomotive, staying with it throughout most of its run, opening the bypass, adjusting the fuel, tapping the throttle, notching up the valve gear? There is a lot to be said for both approaches, and it is up to you to choose the type of engine that best suits your wants.

Looks. Since almost all small scale steam locomotives are manufactured outside of the United States, there are few models of U.S. prototypes available. Also, some of the simple engines are somewhat toylike in appearance.

Don't let this deter you; many of them can be modified to include North American details. But even if they can't be reworked, performance is generally more important than appearance in the garden. Of course, appearance is important—but it is a lot easier to take an engine that runs well and make it look good than it is to take a good-looking engine and try to improve its poor performance.

THE FUTURE

The future of small scale live steam looks bright. Many, many people each year are discovering the joys of running their railroad out of doors, using actual steam as motive power. More and more locomotives are becoming available, and more manufacturers are coming into existence. Why not give serious thought to this exciting new alternative? You won't be alone.

CHAPTER TEN

Technical Information

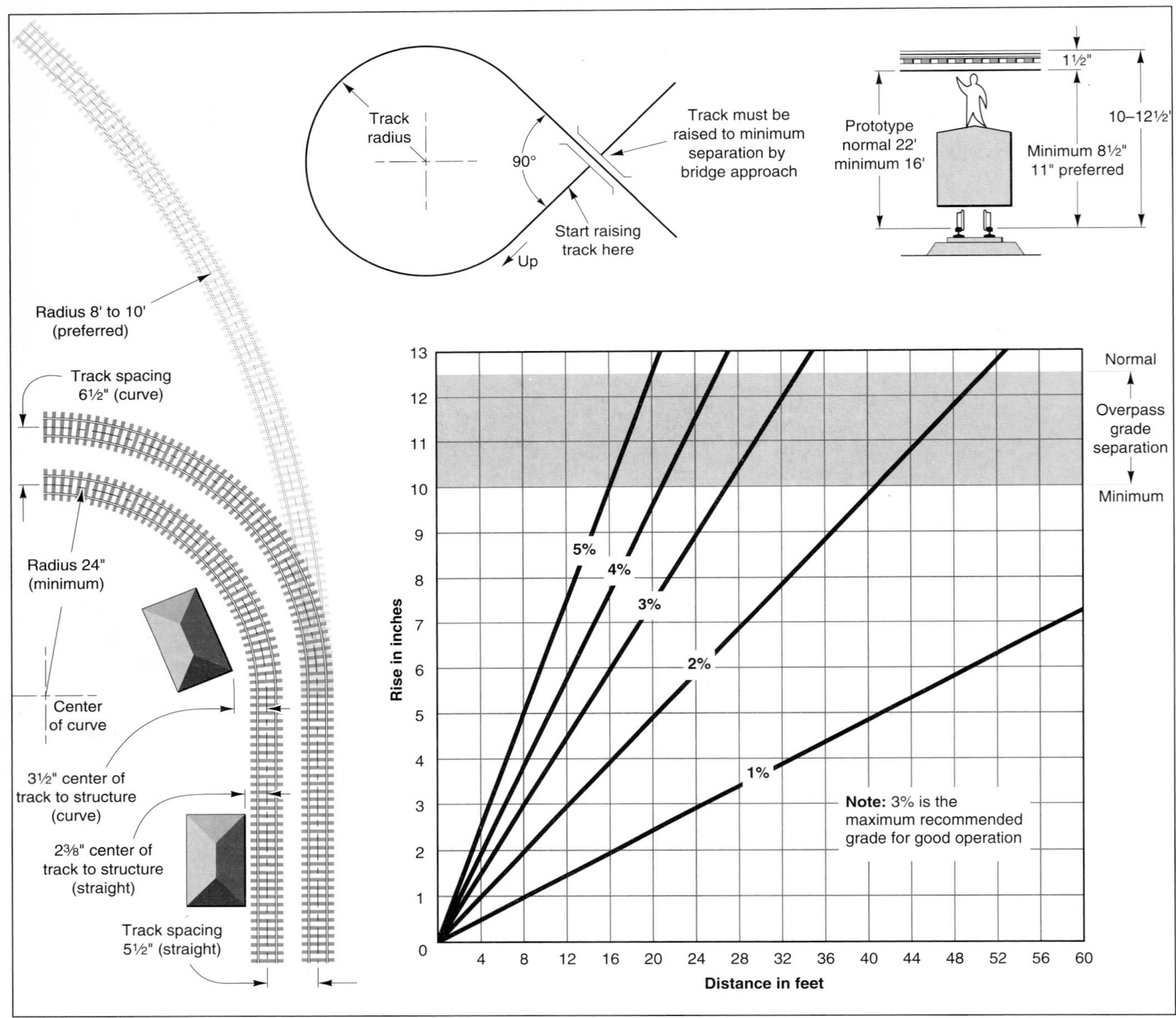

Fig. 10-1. Key track-planning information includes track separation and clearances, left, and grades, right.

When you begin designing your own track plans or altering published ones, you will need to consider grades, track separations, and clearances.

Fig. 10-1 includes key layout-planning information. The radii shown are the standards established by LGB for its sectional track. Radius 1 should be considered the minimum practical radius for any gauge 1 layout. If you have the space, use the largest radii possible. Using flexible track enables you to set your own minimum radius standards for your own layout.

Important clearance information is also shown in **fig. 10-1**. These are based on LGB's track standards and practical experience. It's always a good idea to do some experimenting before you fasten something permanently. Will your favorite locomotive negotiate a tunnel built on a sharp curve? Try it with the tunnel portal temporarily set in place before you build the scenery.

Grades. The grade is simply how steeply the track rises or falls. Perfectly level track has no grade. If you're building an outdoor layout, grades will probably be necessary because the yard won't be flat. With an indoor layout you might want to introduce grades for track-planning considerations or just so your railroad looks like the real ones, which have grades out of necessity.

The important thing to remember about grades is that they reduce the number of cars your locomotive can pull. A 3 percent grade is a 3" rise in 100" (or around 8 feet). That seems fairly gentle, but even a 3 percent grade will cut in half the number of cars your locomotive will be able to pull.

As the grade is increased, you'll reach a point where the locomotive's drivers will spin and it won't even be able to pull itself up. So you want the grades on your layout to be 3 percent or less.

Some magazine product reviews will state how many freight cars a locomotive will pull on straight level track. For large scale locomotives this works out to about one car for each ounce of drawbar pull. So if a locomotive has 10 ounces of drawbar pull, it will be able to pull 10 cars on level track, but only 5 cars if your ruling grade is 3 percent.

If your plan calls for one track to cross over another, you'll have to calculate the grades required so you can raise one or lower the other (or both) to obtain the separation necessary. The information in **fig. 10-1** will help you in figuring grades.

Structure sizes. Another important factor in layout planning is the size of buildings. You'll want to check structure sizes given in catalogs to see how they will fit your plan before making those purchases. You can find this and other track-planning information in a number of sources.

Sources of information. If you're going to get just one reference book for planning purposes, I'd recommend Walthers *World of Large Scale.* This catalog and reference book includes all the large scale equipment and supplies this major distributor carries. While not comprehensive, it shows most large scale equipment offered. It's updated periodically, so the information is current. And it's sold in many hobby shops, so it's easy to find.

You can also write to manufacturers and suppliers for product information. Every major manufacturer has a catalog or product information of some kind. They are listed in the back of this book. Many charge for their catalogs.

One of the nicest and most helpful catalogs is LGB's. The information on track and electrical devices is especially helpful. LGB also publishes a good book, *LGB Track Planning and Technical Guide.* Anyone interested in using LGB components for automatic operation will want this guide.

Other good sources of product information are magazines. Both the advertisements and the product reviews will be helpful to you while you're planning and making purchasing decisions.

SCALE RULES

A scale rule is a handy modeling tool. With one you can measure directly in scale feet. Say you're laying out a single lane road on your G scale layout and you want it to be 8 feet wide. What does 8 feet equal in G scale? You can multiply 8 feet by 12 to get the total number of inches, which is 96, and divide 96 by 22.5. With a calculator, you'll quickly learn that the road should be 4¼" wide.

Using a scale rule, like those printed along the edges of these pages, you simply mark off the road width in scale feet without knowing or caring what the width is in real inches.

The rules printed along the edges of these pages can be cut off or photocopied and mounted on cardstock for temporary use. Once you find out how handy they are for your modeling, you'll want to purchase a commercial one made of metal or plastic.

LARGE SCALE PLANS USING A COPIER

If you want to get into scratchbuilding railroad equipment and structures, you'll need plans to work from. You'll find that hundreds of plans have been published in the smaller modeling scales, especially HO scale. Model railroad magazines are great sources for drawings, but most are published in N, HO, S, or O scales. Most model railroad magazines encourage readers to copy published plans, for their own use, in the scale they're modeling in.

Fig. 10-2 shows the enlargement required to convert smaller scale drawings to large scale. Since the enlargement limit for most copiers is 200%, you'll have to make multiple enlargements in most cases.

	ENLARGEMENT REQUIRED		
Drawing Published in:	No. 1 1:32	1/2" 1:24	G 1:22.5
N 1:160	500%	667%	711%
HO 1:87	272%	363%	387%
S 1:64	200%	267%	284%
O 1:48	150%	200%	213%

Fig. 10-2. Enlarging drawings in smaller scales.

COUPLERS

The European hook-and-loop-style coupler originally used on LGB trains didn't sit well with North American modelers for very long. So the knuckle coupler evolved, with new, original equipment and aftermarket retrofits to replace the hook-and-loop types. There are several different types of knuckle couplers available, and the large

1:24 Scale Rule FEET
0 1 2 3 4 5 6 7 8 9 10 11 12 13 14 15

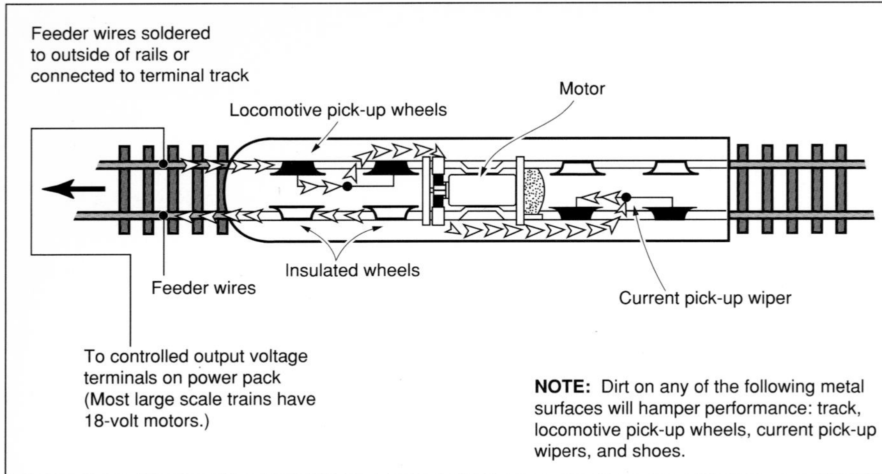

Fig. 10-3. How current flows through a motor.

scale operator will want to settle on a compatible system to ensure trouble-free operation.

BASICS OF WIRING AND TRAIN CONTROL

Wiring doesn't have to be complicated. LGB's track and electrical components make it easy. However, realistic control of your trains and other accessories can take you into some fairly sophisticated control schemes that would take a book to cover. (A good reference book on the subject is Andy Sperandeo's *Your Guide to Easy Model Railroad Wiring.*)

The basic control circuit (12-volt and 18-volt motors). Before we discuss wiring, let's look at the basic control circuit. The track serves both as a guideway for the trains and as the "wires" to the electric motor inside the locomotive. (See **fig. 10-3.**)

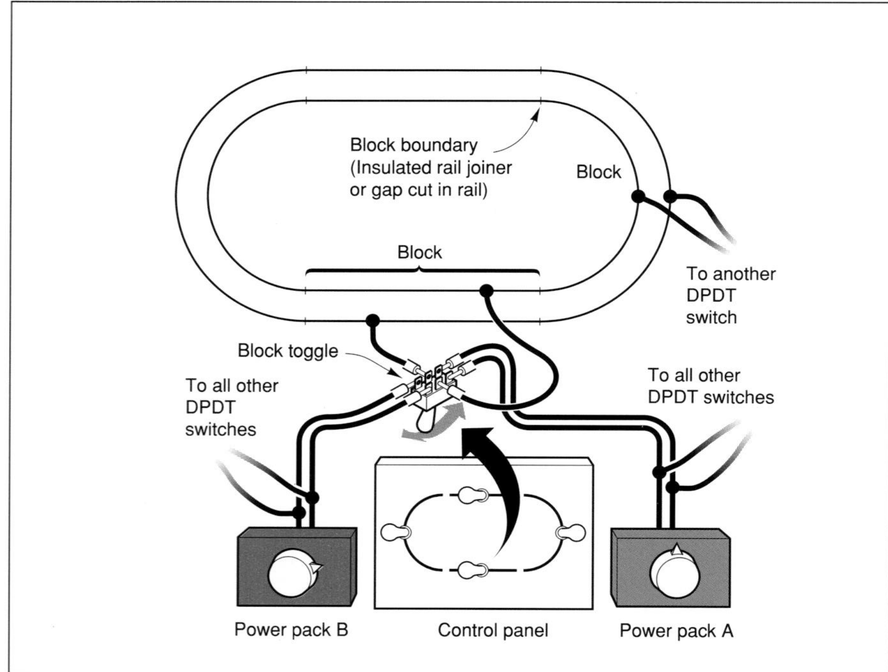

Fig. 10-4. Basics of cab control wiring.

For a locomotive to run smoothly, current must flow from one output terminal of the power pack through a number of rail joiners to the locomotive's pickup wheels to the motor. And that's only half the trip. Nothing happens unless there's a return path through a common rail.

Erratic or jerky operation will result if anything impedes the flow of current through this circuit. The most likely causes will be dirty track or dirty locomotive pickup wheels or shoes. Another likely cause is poor electrical contact through the rail joints.

One-train operation. The simplest wiring scheme is to connect two wires from your power pack to the track. That setup will enable you to run one train anywhere on the layout.

WAYS TO CONTROL TWO OR MORE TRAINS

Separate circuits. If you want to expand your horizons and run more than one train, wiring gets a little more complicated. The most obvious thing to do is to create a separate circuit for the second train. A concentric circle works fine.

Cab control. After watching two trains go round and round, you'll probably want a more realistic form of control—one that allows you to run each of your trains anywhere on the layout under independent control. Cab control is the answer.

Cab control is a basic method of controlling model trains independently. All you need are two power packs and some double-pole, double-throw toggle switches.

The first step is to divide the layout into electrically insulated control blocks. You can create blocks by installing insulated rail as shown in **fig. 10-4.** If you want to establish blocks after the track is laid, you can cut the rail with a razor saw at the block boundaries and glue blocks of .060" styrene in the gaps, so that the rails don't creep back together and touch.

While gapping both rails and

using double-pole, double-throw switches is the easiest concept to understand, it's not really necessary. As you study layout wiring, you'll discover that it's easier to use a common rail return and only gap one rail. The rail sections in the gapped rail (blocks) are then controlled by single-pole, single-throw toggle switches

How cab control works. Fig. 10-5 shows a simple layout with two passing sidings. It's divided into eight blocks. The sequence shows what the two operators have to do to get their trains past one another at one passing siding. As you can see, the toggle switch that controls power to the block is mounted in a corresponding location on the control panel schematic. When each operator's train clears a block, he or she turns the toggle switch for that block to the off position so that the other operator knows the block is available.

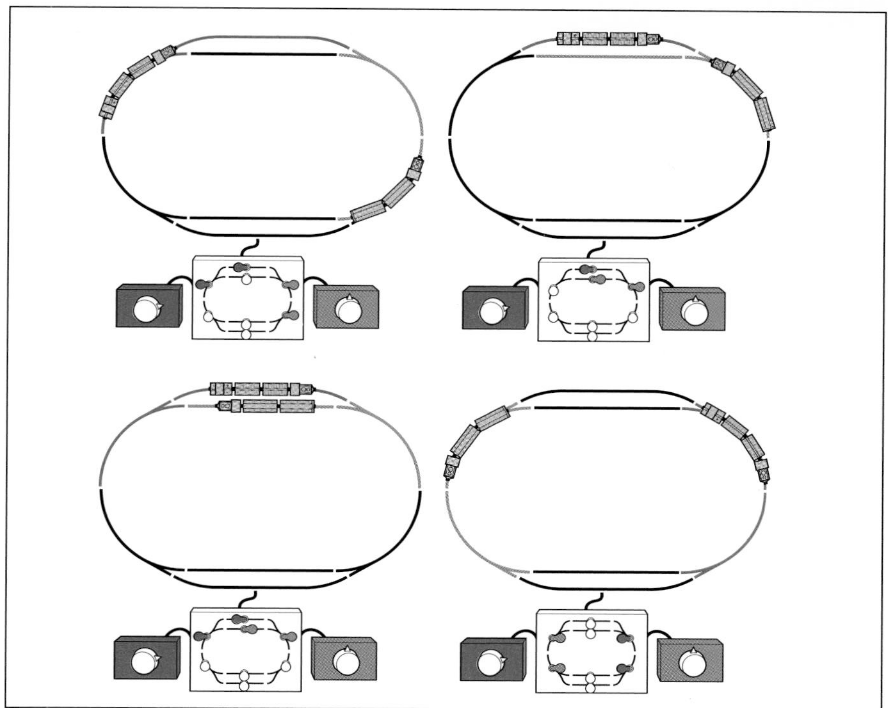

Fig. 10-5. Two trains meet and pass using cab control.

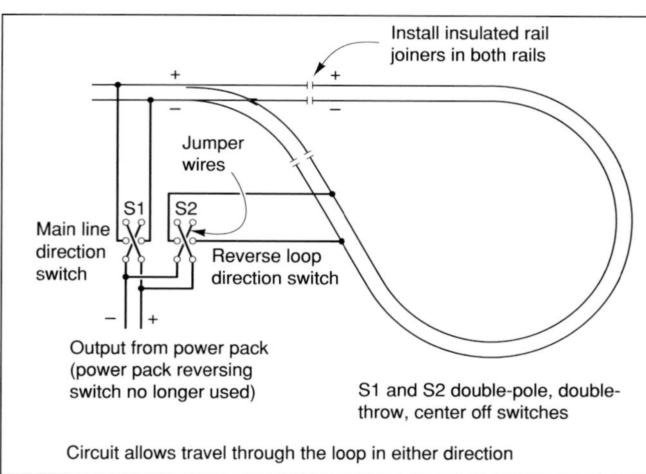

Fig. 10-6. Conventional reverse-loop wiring.

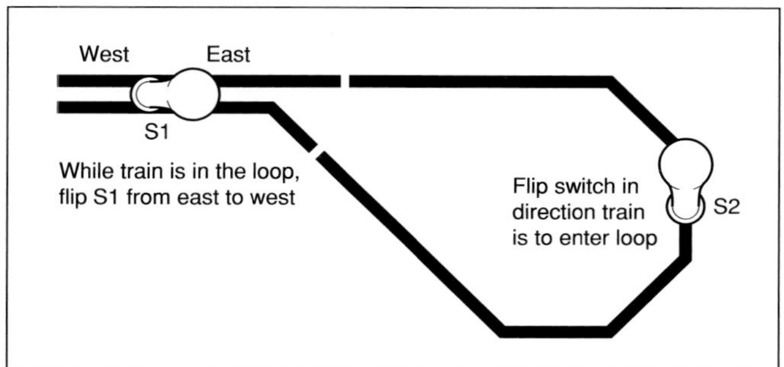

Fig. 10-7. Schematic for reverse loop.

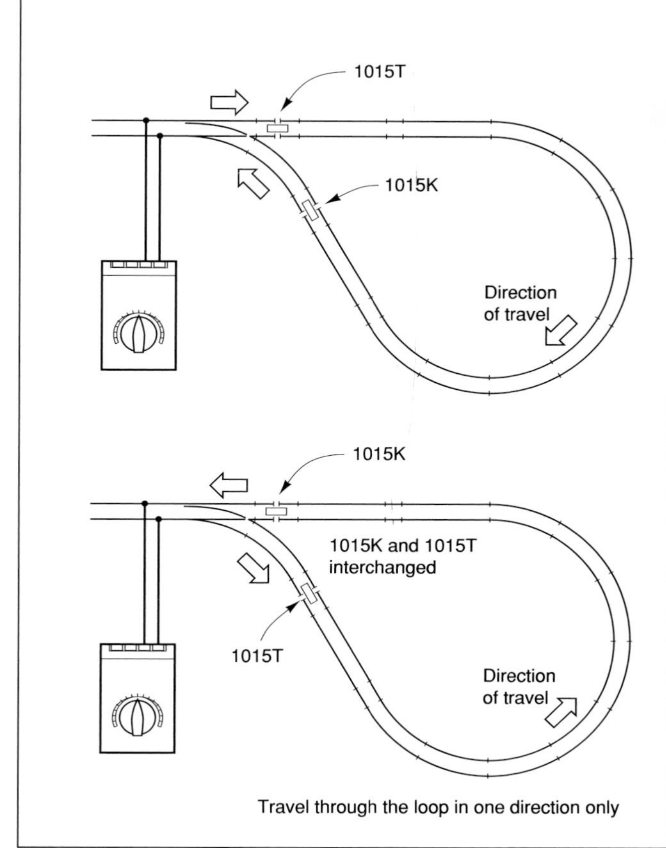

Fig. 10-8. Using LGB components for reverse-loop wiring.

Turning tracks. Any track arrangement that enables a locomotive to reverse direction is called a turning track. The most common turning track is the reverse loop. **Fig. 10-6** shows the conventional way to wire a reverse loop. Note that for reverse loops, both rails must have insulated rail joiners installed or gaps cut.

This conventional system requires the operator to throw two toggle switches each time a train is run through the loop. If you don't mind being restricted to one-directional travel through the loop, LGB has track components that allow automatic operation through reverse loops. Both track sections have the required gaps precut and one section (1015K) contains diodes that restrict the current flow. When connected as shown in **fig. 10-8**, they provide automatic reverse loop operation.

Automatic operation. Automatic operation of trains is popular in Europe. LGB has a line of components for those of you who want to explore this aspect of the hobby. Let's look briefly at the possibilities:

Back and forth operation. The 8009 reversing unit automatically stops a train at the end of a line and, after a preset time, sends it back in the opposite direction. With one of these units at each end of a point-to-point layout you can have the train shuttle back and forth.

Route and block control. The no. 1700 reed switch is mounted between tracks at a strategic location. When a locomotive equipped with a no. 1701 switching magnet passes over it, the contacts close. These contacts can be used to activate the no. 1201 EPL devices and throw switch points. So when the locomotive passes over the reed switch, a turnout ahead is thrown for the proper route for that train. The same principle can be used to control power to other blocks. When one train gets to a selected spot on the layout and passes a no. 1700 switch, power is cut to the block behind, stopping the following train when it gets there.

Command control. Command control is a high-tech approach to operating a number of locomotives under independent control. Instead of the controlling the track power with a power pack knob, the operator controls the locomotive power by means of an electronic device mounted inside each motor driven unit. Full power is always on the track. The amount of power applied to the locomotive's motor is determined by control signals also fed along the rails. The settings of the operator's speed and direction controls determines the speed and direction the locomotive will travel.

Command control is firmly established, and there are many good commercial systems to choose

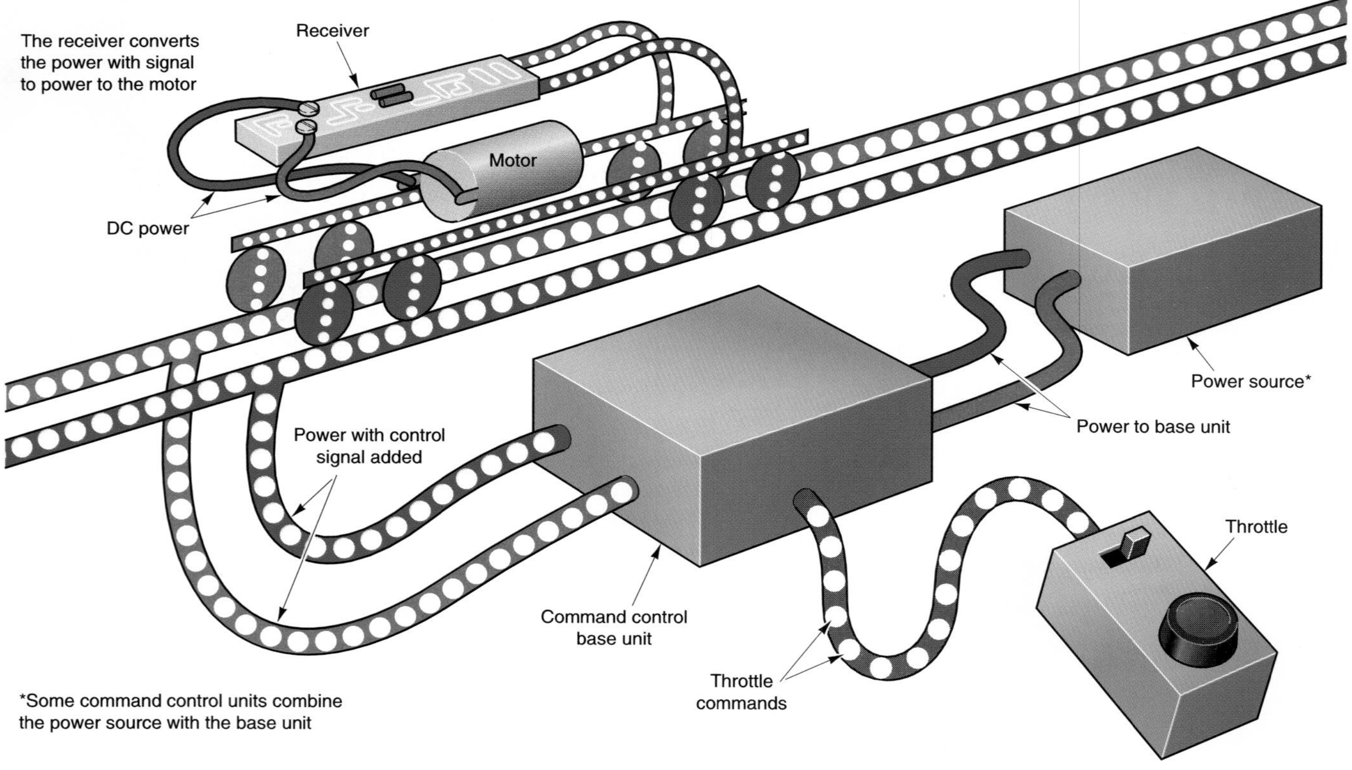

Fig. 10-9. Basic diagram of a command control system.

from. Model railroad magazines review new systems and occasionally do comparative reviews.

The beauty of command control is that trains can be operated just like real ones without any artificial electrical block restrictions. There are no toggles to throw except for turning tracks. The disadvantage is that an electronic control unit, called a receiver or decoder, must be installed in each locomotive. **Fig. 10-9** shows a basic diagram of a command control system.

Radio control. Dirty track is a problem for garden railroaders, so some have gone to radio control and battery power, as discussed in Chapter 6. Several good commercial systems are offered. A typical installation carries the rechargeable batteries and control circuitry in a permanently coupled trailing car, as shown in **fig. 10.**

One disadvantage of radio-controlled battery power is that the weight of the batteries reduces the length of train that the locomotive can pull.

SWITCH MACHINE WIRING

There are two basic ways to throw a turnout's points from side to side. The traditional method, used for many years in the smaller scales, is by a twin coil solenoid. When one coil is energized, an iron rod in the center of the solenoids moves toward that coil. When the other coil is energized, the rod moves back. A linkage between the rod and the switch causes the switch points to move the required distance. Power to energize the solenoids briefly is controlled by single-pole, single-throw, momentary-make push-button switches.

The most common switch machine used in gauge 1 is LGB's, a point motor type. A gear on the shaft of a DC motor rides in a rack, which moves the points back and forth. A double-pole, double-throw (DPDT), momentary-make toggle switch is used to briefly apply power to the motor. LGB's 5075 control box is designed for this task. It controls four switch machines or other accessories. (See **fig. 10-11.**)

You can also purchase DPDT, momentary-make toggle switches and wire them as shown in **fig. 10-12**. The advantage of using individual toggle switches is that you can mount them on a control panel.

MAINTENANCE

Generally speaking, large scale equipment is well made and very reliable. However, locomotive wheels and pickup shoes get dirty, lights burn out, motor brushes wear out, parts break, and metal-to-metal contact surfaces occasionally need lubrication.

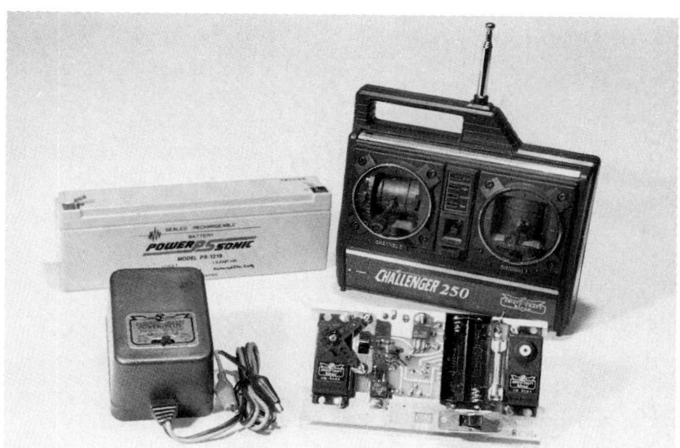

Fig. 10-10. One brand of radio-controlled, battery-powered train control for large scale trains is shown above, left. This system by EDA Electronics consists of an RC transmitter, gell-cell battery, battery charger, and receiver. In the photo above we see the receiver and battery installed in a reefer, which is permanently coupled behind the locomotive. On LGB tenders, left, the connections between the trailing "power car" and the tender can be made via the plugs intended for passenger car lighting. You must also disable the locomotive's track pickups.

1:22.5 Scale Rule
FEET

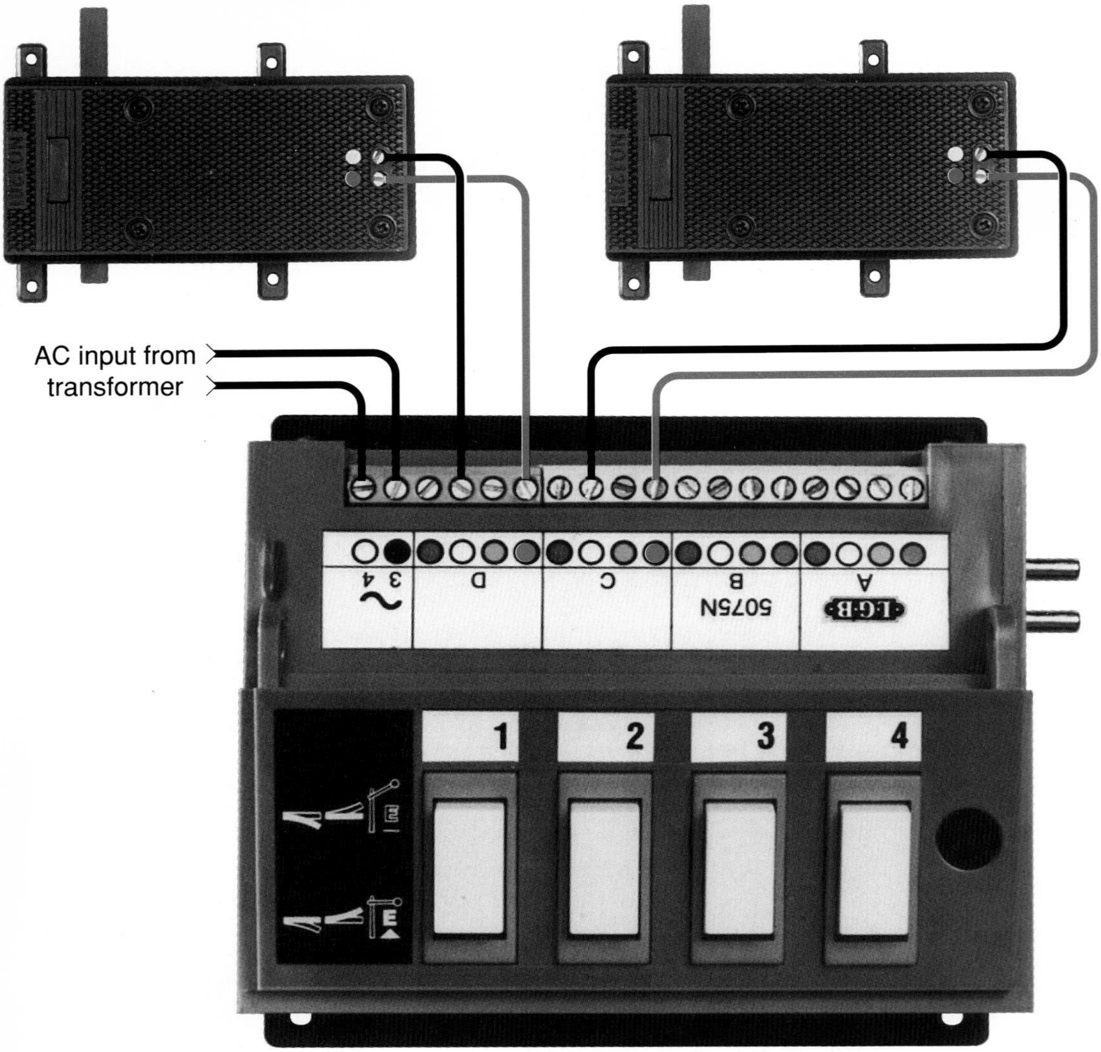

Fig. 10-11. LGB's 5075 control box is commonly used to activate switch machines.

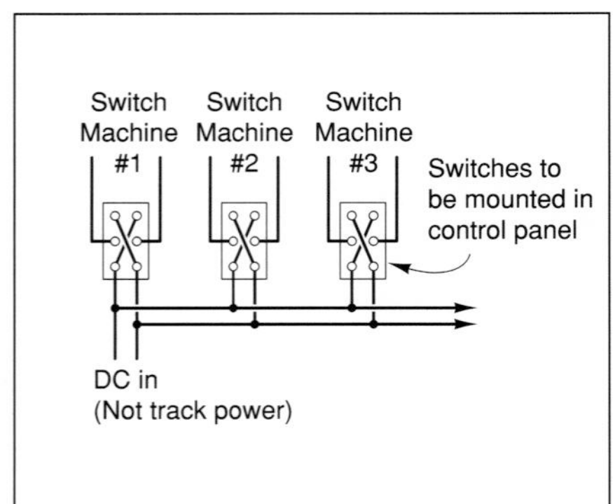

Fig. 10-12. DPDT momentary-make toggle switches can also be used to control switch-machine operations.

Each manufacturer has its own recommendations for maintenance; so it's a good idea to start a file in your shop for maintenance literature supplied with each new purchase, especially locomotives.

For a major repair, especially if it's still covered by warranty, be sure to follow the manufacturer's instructions on how to return the locomotive or other equipment to them.

The repair of an electronic sound unit or a radio control system requires specialized training and test equipment. But before sending it in for repair, do a visual check to see if the problem is something obvious like a broken or loose wire.

An advantage of patronizing a local hobby shop is that they will offer help to their customers; moreover, most have service departments that can help if you can't fix a model yourself.

Suppliers and Organizations

When writing for information, be sure to include a self-addressed, stamped envelope. Some firms offer free catalogs or literature; others charge for their catalogs. Some large scale railroad suppliers will sell direct to consumers; others sell only through hobby shops. Always check with your local hobby shop before attempting to order direct from a manufacturer or importer. If you don't have a hobby shop in your area, there a number of firms that sell large scale equipment by mail order.

Aristo-Craft
Polk's Model Craft Hobbies Inc.
346 Bergen Ave.
Jersey City, NJ 07304
Gauge 1 track plus a complete line of 1:29 scale locomotives, cars, and accessories

Bachmann Industries, Inc.
1400 East Erie Ave.
Philadelphia, PA 19124
Complete line of Gn3 products, including locomotives, cars, track, power packs, train sets, and accessories

***Classic Toy Trains* Magazine**
21027 Crossroads Circle
P. O. Box 1612
Waukesha, WI 53187
Leading magazine for toy train collectors and operators. New product reporting of large scale and occasional features on large scale.

Coronado Scale Models
1544 E. Cypress St.
Phoenix, AZ
Mail order source for ½" scale kits and parts for scratchbuilding

Depot G Hobbies
371 Florida Ln.
Winfield, IL 60190
Structure kits and freight car loads

Eastern Railways
RD 1, Box 254
Beech Creek, PA 16822
Importer of handcrafted brass locomotives and cars in No. 1 scale

***Garden Railways* Magazine**
P. O. Box 61461
Denver, CO 80206
Bimonthly magazine serving the hobby of garden railroading. See the latest issue of *Garden Railways* magazine for up-to-date information on garden railway clubs

Garich Light Transport
6101 Glenwood Dr.
Huntington Beach, CA 92647
Gauge 1 track, turnout kits, rail, spikes, tie plates, dual-gauge track (0 and 1)

Grandt Line Products Inc.
1040 Shary Ct.
Concord, CA 94518
Manufacturer of ½" plastic scale windows, doors and other parts for scratchbuilding structures

Kadee Quality Products Co.
673 Ave. C
White City, OR 97503
Knuckle couplers for large scale that can be uncoupled over magnetic uncoupling ramps

LGB of America
6444 Nancy Ridge Dr.
San Diego, CA 92121
U.S. office of German firm Ernst Paul Lehmann, which invented G scale in 1968. Company offers a complete line of Gn3 equipment, including locomotives, cars, track, figures, power packs, and accessories.

LGB Model Railroad Club, Inc.
P. O. Box 15835
Pittsburgh, PA 15244-5835
Association of LGB fans publishes a magazine and sponsors an annual convention

Lionel Trains, Inc.
26750 Twenty-Three Mile Rd.
Mt. Clemens, MI 48045
Manufacturer of No. 1 scale locomotives, cars, and track

Micro Engineering Company
1120 Eagle Rd.
Fenton, MO 63026
Gauge 1 track and turnouts sold under the G-TRAK brand name

Miniature Plant Kingdom
4125 Harrison Grade Rd.
Sebastopol, CA 95472
Source for miniature trees and flowers suitable for garden railroads

The Miniatures Catalog
Kalmbach Miniatures Inc.
P. O. Box 1612
Waukesha, WI 53187
Source guide to dollhouse miniatures hobby. Includes ½" scale structures and detail parts, which can be used for G scale.

Model Die Casting, Inc.
P. O. Box 1927
Carson City, NV 89702
Gn3 locomotives and freight cars, 1:32 scale freight cars

***Model Railroader* Magazine**
21027 Crossroads Circle
P. O. Box 1612
Waukesha, WI 53187
Leading model railroad magazine, serving all scales

Model Rectifier Corp. (MRC)
2500 Woodbridge Avenue
Edison, NJ 08817
Power packs

National Model Railroad Association (NMRA)
4121 Cromwell Rd.
Chattanooga, TN 37421
International association of model railroad hobbyists. Organization sets industry standards, publishes a monthly magazine, and sponsors local meets and regional and national conventions. Write for current annual membership fee.

Nicholas Smith Trains
2343 West Chester Pike
Broomall, PA 19008
Mail order source for large scale trains

NorthWest Short Line
Box 423
Seattle, WA 98111
Motors, gears, special tools, gauge 1 power trucks

***Outdoor Railroader* Magazine**
1574 Kerryglen Street
Westlake, CA 91361
Bimonthly magazine devoted to large scale railroading outdoors.

Ozark Miniatures
P. O. Box 22
Linn Creek, MO 65052
G scale logging equipment and detail parts

Playmobil USA Inc.
11-E Nicholas Ct.
Dayton, NJ 08810
Toy manufacturer whose line includes large scale trains, sets, and accessories for young children (LGB compatible)

Pola
8734 Rothhausen
Germany
Manufacturer of G scale structures

Preiser
Steinfield Postfach 12-33
D-8803, Rottenburg, Germany
Extensive line of G scale and some No. 1 scale (1:32) figures of people and animals, plus detail items

San-Val Trains
7444 Valjean Ave.
Van Nuys, CA 91406
Mail order source for large scale trains. Manufactures gauge 1 wheelsets, track-cleaning devices, and screw-on rail joiners

Sidestreet Bannerworks
P. O. Box 61461
Denver, CO 80206
Videotapes on garden railroading, gauge 3 freight car trucks, and small scale live-steam locomotives

***Steam in the Garden* Magazine**
P. O. Box 335
Newark Valley, NY 13811
Publication dedicated exclusively to small scale live-steam locomotives operated on garden railways.

USA Trains
P. O. Box 100
Malden, MA 02148
Manufacturer of a line of Gn3 freight cars

Watts' Train Shop
9180 Hunt Club Rd.
Zionsville, IN 46077
Mail order source for G scale trains

West Lawn Locomotive Works
P. O. Box 570
Madison, WI 53701
Source for gauge 1 live steam locomotives

William K. Walthers, Inc.
P. O. Box 18676
Milwaukee, WI 53218
Manufacturer and distributor of model railroad products in all scales. Publishes a catalog and reference manual, *The World of Large Scale Trains,* which lists most products offered.

Index

A
Automatic train operation, 92

B
Backdrops, 39
  construction of, 31
Ballast, types of, 53
Ballasting track
  indoor layouts, 36
  outdoor layouts, 68
Benchwork, 32

C
Cab control explained, 90
Cleaning wheels, 25
Clearances, 88
Clockwork trains, 56
Collecting large scale trains, 27
Colorado & Western RR track plan, 45
Command control, 92
Concept for a model railroad explained, 30
Control panel construction, 38
Copier, how to use to enlarge plans, 89
Crusher fines for ballast, 53
Cutting rail, 36
Cylinder, oscillating, 83

D
Detailing a layout, 40

E
Ernst Paul Lehmann Patentwerk (LGB), 2

F
Ferrocement for outdoor scenery, 69
Flexible track, 50

G
G scale, 4
Garden railroading, 27, 48
  choosing equipment, 49
  planning considerations, 49
  wiring, 54
Garden railways, a history of, 7
Gauge, explanation of, 3
Gauge 1, 3
Gn3, 4
Grades
  how to calculate, 89
  how they reduce pulling power, 89
Ground foam, uses for, 39

H
Handlaying track for outdoor use, 51
Hardshell scenery, 39
History of toy and model trains, 5
Homasote roadbed, 43

I
Illusions using mirrors, 40
Impatiens, Begonia & Northern track plan, 64

K
Kadee couplers, 47

L
Landscaping a garden railroad, 56
Layout planning information, 88
LGB, 8, 43
L-girder benchwork, 32
Lionel, 6
Live steam, history of, 81
Live steamers, 8
Locomotive wheel cleaning, 25

M
Maintenance tips, 24
Märklin, 6
Mirrors, uses of, 40
Modeling scales compared, 3
Mulch, uses for, 57
Muskego & Western track plan, 29

N
Narrow gauge, explanation of, 3
Narrow gauge layout, 26
No. 1 scale explained, 4

P
Plans, how to enlarge using a photocopier, 89
Plants for garden railroads, 72
  selection for garden railroad use, 60, 61
Ponds, methods of building, 70
Power pack, how to connect to track, 15

R
Radio control
  for electric locomotives, 55, 93
  for steam locomotives, 85
Rail, how to cut, 36
Reverse loop wiring, 38, 91
Roadbed
  for indoor layouts, 34
  for outdoor layouts, 52, 65
Rock castings, 39
Room preparation, 31

S
Scale rules, 89
Scales explained, 3
Scenery
  how to build indoors, 39
  how to build outdoors, 69
Scratchbuilding locomotives, 45
Sectional track, 50
Small scale live steam, definition of, 81
Standard gauge, 3, 26
Steam cylinder, how it works, 82
Steam engine
  cutaway of, 82
  how to operate, 84
Surveying a yard for a garden railroad, 65
Switch machine wiring, 93
Switching problem, how to solve, 21

T
Texturing process for scenery, 39
Track
  cleaning, 24
  fastening to roadbed, 19, 35
  flexible, 50
  handlaying for outdoor use, 51
  sectional, 50
  sizes explained, 50
  tracklaying outdoors, 68
Track-planning template, 18
Track plans for beginners, 16, 17
Train control methods, 73, 90
Train sets, 14
Tree construction methods, 43
Turning tracks, 92
Turnout control, 38, 94

V
Valve gear, description of, 83

W
Wiring a layout, 15, 37, 67, 90